LIVERPOOL EVERYMAN AND PLAYHOUSE
PRESENT THE WORLD PREMIÈRE OF

THE WAY HOME

BY CHLOË MOSS

FIRST PERFORMED AT THE
EVERYMAN THEATRE, LIVERPOOL
FRIDAY 20 OCTOBER 2006

LIVERPOOL EVERYMAN AND PLAYHOUSE

About the Theatres

As Liverpool prepares to take on the mantle of European Capital of Culture in 2008, the Everyman and Playhouse are experiencing a dramatic upsurge in creative activity. Since January 2004, we have been continually in production, creating shows which have ensured that 'Made in Liverpool' is widely recognised as a stamp of theatrical quality once again.

Around our in-house productions, we host some of the finest touring companies from around the country, to offer a rich and varied programme for the people of Liverpool and Merseyside, and for the increasing number of visitors to our city.

But there is more to these theatres than simply the work on our stages. We have a busy Literary Department, working to nurture the next generation of Liverpool Playwrights. A wide-ranging Community Department takes our work to all corners of the city and surrounding areas, and works in partnership with schools, colleges, youth and community groups to open up the theatre to all.

Our aim is for these theatres to be an engine for creative excellence, artistic adventure, and audience involvement; firmly rooted in our community, yet both national and international in scope and ambition.

"The two theatres have undergone a remarkable renaissance… Liverpool's theatreland has not looked so good for years" Daily Post

Liverpool Everyman and Playhouse is a registered charity no.1081229
www.everymanplayhouse.com

Liverpool Everyman and Playhouse would like to thank all our current funders:

Corporate Members A C Robinson and Associates, Barbara McVey, Beetham Organisation, Benson Signs, Brabners Chaffe Street, Chadwick Chartered Accountants, Downtown Liverpool in Business, Duncan Sheard Glass, DWF Solicitors, EEF NorthWest, Grant Thornton, Hope Street Hotel, Mando Group, Morgenrot Chevaliers, Nviron Ltd, Synergy Colour Printing, The Mersey Partnership, Victor Huglin Carpets

Trusts & Grant-Making Bodies
BBC Radio Merseyside, The Eleanor Rathbone Charitable Trust, The Harry Pilkington Trust, The Golsoncott Foundation, The Granada Foundation, Liverpool Culture Company, The Lynn Foundation, The Peggy Ramsey Foundation, Penny Cress Trust, PH Holt Charitable Trust, The Pilkington General Fund, The Rex Makin Charitable Trust, The Garrick Trust, The Julia Marmor Trust, The Ernest Cook Trust, Malcolm and Roger Frood in memory of Graham and Joan Frood.

This theatre has the support of the Pearson's Playwrights' Scheme sponsored by Pearson plc. Assisted by Business in the Arts: North West

Individual Supporters Peter and Geraldine Bounds, George C Carver, Councillor Eddie Clein, Mr and Mrs Dan Hugo, A.Thomas Jackson, Ms D Leach, Frank D Paterson, Les Read, Sheena Streather, Frank D Thompson, DB Williams and all those who prefer to remain anonymous.

NEW WRITING AT THE LIVERPOOL EVERYMAN AND PLAYHOUSE

"The Everyman is back producing the next generation of Liverpool playwrights"
(The Guardian)

At the beating heart of the theatre's renaissance is our work with writers; since it is our passionate belief that an investment in new writing is an investment in our theatrical future.

The Way Home is the latest in a rich and varied slate of world, european or regional premières which has been enthusiastically received by Merseyside audiences and helped to put Liverpool's theatre back on the national map.

"a stunning theatrical coup"
(Liverpool Echo on *Unprotected*)

Highly acclaimed productions have included the European première of *Yellowman* by Dael Orlandersmith, which transferred to Hampstead Theatre and successfully toured nationally in spring 2006, and regional premières of Conor McPherson's *Port Authority*, Simon Block's *Chimps* and Gregory Burke's *On Tour* - a co-production with London's Royal Court. And in just over two years, the theatres will have produced six world premières of plays developed and nurtured in Liverpool - *Fly* by Katie Douglas; *The Kindness of Strangers* by Tony Green; *Urban Legend* by Laurence Wilson, *The Morris* by Helen Blakeman; *Unprotected* by Esther Wilson, John Fay, Tony Green, Lizzie Nunnery, which transferred to the Edinburgh festival where it won the Amnesty International Freedom of Speech Award, and *Paradise Bound* by Jonathan Larkin.

"A remarkable renaissance"
(Liverpool Daily Post)

Around the main production programme, the theatres run a range of projects and activities to create opportunities and offer support to writers at every career stage. The commissioning programme invests in the creation of new work for both the Everyman and the Playhouse stages.

The Young Writer's Programme is a year long programme working alongside experienced practitioners, which nurtures and develops exciting new voices to create a new generation of Liverpool writers. An annual new writing festival, Everyword, offers a busy and popular week of seminars, sofa talks and work-in-progress readings.

"Laurence Wilson is another name to add to the theatre's long and glorious reputation for nurturing new talent"
(Liverpool Echo on *Urban Legend*)

For more information about the Everyman and Playhouse - including the full programme, off-stage activities such as playwright support, and ways in which you can support our investment in talent - visit www.everymanplayhouse.com.

CREDITS

THE CAST (IN ALPHABETICAL ORDER)

Ang Thompson — Leanne Best
Margaret O'Driscoll — Claire Cogan
Felix O'Connor — Luke Hayden
Ellie O'Connor — Amy Mc Allister
Paul Thompson — Nick Moss
Daniel O'Connor — Eamonn Owens
Bobby Thompson — Joe Shipman

THE COMPANY

Writer	Chloë Moss
Director	Sue Dunderdale
Designer	Bob Bailey
Lighting Designer	Tina MacHugh
Sound Designer	Sean Pritchard
Assistant Director	Gemma Kerr
Costume Supervisor	Jacquie Davies
Dialect Coach	Joe Taylor
Production Manager	Emma Wright
Stage Manager	Natalia Cortes
Deputy Stage Manager	Emma Hay
Assistant Stage Manager	Maria Wells
Wardrobe Mistress	Marie Jones
Lighting Operators	Marc Williams
	Dave Sherman
Sound Operator	Lindsey Bell
Stage Crew	Howard Macauley
	Andy Webster
Set Construction	Splinter
Dramaturg	Suzanne Bell

approx running time: act one 45 minutes interval act two 1 hour 5 minutes

CAST

LEANNE BEST
ANG THOMPSON

Leanne's theatre credits include:
Unprotected (Traverse Theatre,
Edinburgh); *34* (Fecund Theatre
Company); *The Morris, Macbeth*
and *Unprotected* (Liverpool
Everyman); *Solitary Confinement*
(King's Head Theatre); *Popcorn*
(Liverpool Playhouse); *Julius
Caesar, Nicholas Nickleby, Live
Like Pigs, Our Country's Good,
Platanov, Macbeth* and *The
Crucible* (LIPA).

Television includes: *Casualty,
Heatwave, Wire in the Blood,
Memory of Water, Casbah - A
Documentary, New Street Law* and
forthcoming drama *Mobile.*

Radio includes: *The Importance
of Being Earnest.*

Leanne has also participated in
rehearsed readings and workshops
for new writing at the Liverpool
Everyman's Everyword festival, the
Actor's Centre, the Young Vic and
The Royal Court Theatre, London.

CLAIRE COGAN
MARGARET O'DRISCOLL

Claire's Theatre Credits Include:
The Mysteries (Belgrade Theatre,
Coventry); *Head/Case* (The Swan
and Soho Theatre); *Freedom of
The City* (Finborough Theatre,
London); *Factory Girls* (Lyric
Theatre, Belfast); *The Threepenny
Opera* (Bruiser Theatre Company);
Charlotte's Web (Lyric Theatre)
and *Lags* (Battersea Arts Centre
and Theatre 503).

Film Includes: *Chihuahua, Wild
About Harry* and *The Most Fertile
Man In Ireland.*

Television Includes:
The McKeever Show and
Everything You Know Is Wrong.

LUKE HAYDEN
FELIX O'CONNOR

Luke's theatre credits include:
Hamlet (Cork Opera House);
The Field (Tour); *The Hostage*
(Tricycle Theatre, London); *Boris
Godunov* (Covent Garden Opera
House); *The Shadow of a
Gunman* (Falcon Theatre, London);
Oliver (Helix Theatre, Dublin); *The
Merchant of Venice* (Tour);
La Chunga and *Tearing The Loom*
(Lyric Theatre, Belfast); *I Do Not
Like Thee Doctor Fell* and
Educating Rita (Andrew's Lane,
Dublin); *She Stoops To Conquer*
(Gate Theatre, Dublin); *Buried
Child* (Focus Theatre, Dublin) and
The Iceman Cometh (Abbey
Theatre, Dublin).

Television includes: *Fair City,
Fear Anphoist, Father Ted, Poirot,
The Governor, Making Ends Meet,
Casualty* and *The New Adventures
of Robin Hood.*

Film includes: *Veronica Guerin,
The Escapist, Coolockland, One
Man's Hero, Michael Collins* and
In The Name of The Father.

AMY Mc ALLISTER
ELLIE O'CONNOR

Amy studied at The Guildhall
School of Music and Drama where
she appeared in productions of
*Oh What A Lovely War!, Tale of
Two Cities, Cinderella, Twelfth
Night, Measure For Measure,
She Loves Me, Trojan Women,
The Norman Conquests,
The Country Wife* and *The
Seagull.* She has also appeared
in a Royal Court production of
Live Like Pigs.

NICK MOSS
PAUL THOMPSON

Nick's theatre credits include: *Urban Legend, The Mayor of Zalamea* and *Scouse* (Liverpool Everyman); *Coming Around Again, Enjoy* and *Huddersfield* (West Yorkshire Playhouse); *The People Are Friendly, Made of Stone* and *Naturalised* (Royal Court Theatre, London); *An Evening With Gary Lineker* (Oldham Coliseum); *The Snow Queen* (Library Theatre, Manchester); *A Man From The Motor Show* (Unity Theatre, Liverpool) and *Having A Ball* and *Man of The Moment* (Theatre Royal, York).

Television includes: *Coronation Street, The Bill, Casualty, Paradise Heights, Smack The Pony, Mersey Beat, Casualty, Doctors, Always & Everyone, Liverpool One, Lifeforce, Heartbeat, City Central, Cops, Retrace, Hillsborough, Police 2020* and *Emmerdale.*

Film includes: *Trauma, The Calcium Kid, Mean Machine, Al's Lads, Going Off Big Time* and *Heart.*

EAMONN OWENS
DANIEL O'CONNOR

Eamonn studied Acting at Trinity College, Dublin.

Eamonn's theatre credits include: *Beauty Queen of Leenane* (Livin Dread Theatre Company); *Tadhg Stray Wandered In* (Fishamble Theatre Company) and *The Field* (Tricycle Theatre Company).

Television includes: *Big Bow Wow, Bachelors Walk, Benedict Arnold, The Fitz, St. Patrick* and *Amongst Women.*

Film includes: *Studs, My Family Tree, Breakfast on Pluto, The Boys From County Clare, Magdalene Sisters, The Seventh Stream, The Terms, Angela's Ashes, The Butcher Boy* and *The General.*

COMPANY

JOE SHIPMAN
BOBBY THOMPSON

Joe studied at the Liverpool Arts Centre before undertaking actors training at the University of Wales, Aberystwyth. He also trained on Hope Street's Physical Theatre Programme.

Joe's theatre credits include:
Wrong Place Right Time (Contact Theatre, Manchester); *Free To Do As I Say, Macbeth, Life is...* and *The Trial* (Unity Theatre, Liverpool); *Lord of The Flies* and *Little Shop of Horrors* (Campion Theatre); *Greek, Electra* and *Chilli Disks Launch* (Liverpool Arts Centre); *Rollercoaster* (Tour); *Popcorn* and *Then...* (Aberystwyth Arts Centre).

CHLOË MOSS
WRITER

Chloë's first play *Day in Dull Armour* was produced by the Royal Court Theatre, for which she won the Young Writers Festival, 2002. Her second play *How Love is Spelt* was produced at the Bush Theatre, London Autumn 2004 and received its US première at the Summer Play Festival, New York, 2005.

Chloë was writer-in-residence at the Bush Theatre, London during 2003 and Paines Plough during 2004. She has recently finished an attachment at The National Theatre and is under commission by Paines Plough Theatre Company, the Royal Court Theatre and Clean Break.

Chloë's latest play, *Christmas is Miles Away*, premièred at the Manchester Royal Exchange in November, 2005 and transferred to the Bush Theatre in 2006. Chloë is also currently writing a one hour film for the BBC Decades project.

SUE DUNDERDALE
DIRECTOR

Recent theatre credits include:
Paradise Bound (Liverpool Everyman); *Mrs Pat* (York Theatre Royal); *Bottle Universe* (The Bush Theatre); *Cold Hands* (Theatre 503, Battersea); *Squint* (The Chelsea Theatre); *Killing the Cat* (Royal Court Theatre); *The House of Yes* (Soho Theatre Company); *Teendreams* (The Guildhall School of Drama); *Deborah's Daughter* (Library Theatre, Manchester); *The Land of the Living* (Royal Court Upstairs) and *The Water Children* (National Theatre Studio).

Television credits include:
Eastenders, Nativity Blues, Brookside, Coronation Street, Emmerdale, Casualty, The Bill, Heartbeat, Space Island One, The Blood That's In You, London Bridge, Justice and *Rockface.*

Sue has recently written and directed a short film *Last Laugh* which has been invited to play at a variety of film festivals including Los Angeles and Chicago. She is also Head of Directing at RADA.

BOB BAILEY
DESIGNER

Bob's theatre credits include:
Paradise Bound (Liverpool Everyman); *Love Me Tonight* (Hampstead); *The Lying Kind* (Royal Court, London); *Edward Gant's Amazing Feats of Loneliness* (The Drum, Plymouth); *Angels In America* and *Charley's Aunt* (Crucible Theatre, Sheffield); *Bottle Universe, The God Botherers, Stitching, Hijra* and *Pumpgirl* (Bush Theatre, London); *All Nighter* (The Royal Ballet); *Rent* and *Cabaret* (English Theatre, Frankfurt); *Translations* and *Moll Flanders* (Theatre Royal, Bristol Old Vic) and UK Tours of *Anything Goes, The New Statesman, Lieutenant of Inishmore* and *The Real Thing.*

Opera includes: *Don Giovanni* (British Youth Opera), *Manon Lescaut, Fedora, Macbeth* and *La Sonnambula* (Opera Holland Park); *Falstaff* (Guildhall Opera); *Tosca* (Nationale Reisopera, Netherlands); *About Face* (Linbury Theatre, Royal Opera House).

In 1999 Bob was awarded Time Out Designer of The Year for his Set Design for DV8's production of *The Happiest Day Of My Life* (UK and European Tour).

TINA MacHUGH
LIGHTING DESIGNER

Tina recently lit *Paradise Bound* for the Everyman and *Mrs Pat* (York Theatre Royal) both directed by Sue Dunderdale. She has also just lit *The Grapes of Wrath* (Clwyd Theatr Cymru); *The Alice Trilogy* (Abbey, Dublin); *Ubu Roi* (Galway Arts Festival) and future plans include *La Boheme* and *A Streetcar Named Desire* (Opera Ireland) and *Sleeping Beauty* (Helix Theatre, Dublin). As well as many other productions in Ireland she has worked extensively in the UK including productions for the Royal Court, Royal Exchange and in the West End as well as the national tour of *When Harry Met Sally*. She also works regularly in Dance and Opera and most recently on *Apollo* and *Hyacinthus* (Opera Theatre Company, Dublin/Classical Opera UK tour); *Alcina* and *Falstaff* (English Touring Opera); *Idomeneo* (LA Opera with Placido Domingo) and a new dance piece *00:00:00:00: Timecode* (Royal Opera House Clore Studio).

For the RSC she lit *The Tempest*, *Love In A Wood*, *The Comedy of Errors*, *Henry VI* and *Ghosts* (Olivier Award nomination) as well as *Guiding Star* and *Rutherford and Son* (also Olivier Award nomination) for The National.

SEAN PRITCHARD
SOUND DESIGNER

Sean is from Liverpool and studied Production and Performance Technology at The Liverpool Institute for Performing Arts before taking a job with the Everyman Theatre in 1999 where he served as Chief Technician. He is currently Senior Production Manager at the Everyman and Playhouse.

Sound designs for the company include: *Paradise Bound, Port Authority, Urban Legend, The Kindness of Strangers, Fly, The Mayor of Zalamea, A Little Pinch of Chilli, 'Master Harold'… and the Boys, The Tempest, Cinderella, the Rock 'n' Roll panto* and the recent UK tour of *Yellowman*.

GEMMA KERR
ASSISTANT DIRECTOR

Gemma is from Liverpool and has just completed the MFA Theatre Directing course at Birkbeck, University of London. For the past year she has been working as resident Assistant Director at Southwark Playhouse.

Gemma's directing credits include: *Hitting Town* (Southwark Playhouse) and *People In Gingerbread Houses Shouldn't Throw Pasties* (Alma Tavern, Bristol).

Assisting directing credits include: *The Beauty Queen of Leenane* (Watford Palace Theatre); *Beasts and Beauties* (Bristol Old Vic) and *The Canterbury Tales* (Southwark Playhouse).

JACQUIE DAVIES
COSTUME SUPERVISOR

Jacquie's theatre credits include: *The Morris* and *Port Authority* (Liverpool Everyman); *Vurt, Wise Guys, Unsuitable Girls* and *Perfect* (Contact Theatre, Manchester); *Oleanna* (Clwyd Theatr Cymru); *Love on the Dole* (Lowry); *Never the Sinner* (Library Theatre) and *Shockheaded Peter* (West End).

Opera includes work at: Scottish Opera, Buxton Opera Festival, Music Theatre Wales and Opera Holland Park.

Television and film includes: *Queer as Folk II, The Parole Officer, I Love The 1970's and 1980's, Brookside* and *Hollyoaks*.

COMPANY THANKS
Abbey Cycles
Create
Sony Computer Entertainment UK

STAFF

Leah Abbott Box Office Assistant Vicky Adlard Administrator, Laura Arends Marketing Campaigns Manager, Deborah Aydon Executive Director, Jane Baxter Box Office Manager, Rob Beamer Chief Electrician (Playhouse), Lindsey Bell Technician, Suzanne Bell Literary Manager, Gemma Bodinetz Artistic Director, Emma Callan Cleaning Staff, Moira Callaghan Theatre and Community Administrator, Colin Carey Security Officer, Nicole Collarbone Box Office Assistant, Joe Cornmell Finance Assistant, Angela Dooley Cleaning Staff, Alison Eley Finance Assistant, Roy Francis Maintenance Technician, Melanie Gilbert Stage Door/Receptionist, Rosalind Gordon Deputy Box Office Manager, Carl Graceffa Bar Supervisor, Mike Gray Deputy Technical Stage Manager, Helen Griffiths Deputy House Manager, Jayne Gross Development Manager, Stuart Holden IT and Communications Manager, Alison Jones Interim General Manager, David Jordan Fire Officer, Sarah Kelly Assistant House Manager, Sue Kelly Cleaning Staff, Steven Kennett Assistant Maintenance Technician (Performance), Sven Key Fire Officer, Lynn-Marie Kilgallon Internal Courier, Gavin Lamb Marketing Communications Officer, Rachel Littlewood Community Outreach Co-ordinator, Robert Longthorne Building Development Director, Howard Macauley Deputy Chief Technician (Stage), Ged Manson Cleaning Staff, Peter McKenna Cleaning Staff, Jason McQuaide Technical Stage Manager (Playhouse), Kirstin Mead Development Officer, Liz Nolan Assistant to the Directors, Lizzie Nunnery Literary Assistant, Sarah Ogle Marketing Director, Sue Parry Theatres Manager, Sean Pritchard Senior Production Manager, Collette Rawlinson Stage Door/Receptionist, Victoria Rope Programme Co-ordinator, Rebecca Ross-Willams Theatre and Community Director, Jeff Salmon Technical Director, Steve Sheridan Assistant Maintenance Technician, Jackie Skinner Education Co-ordinator, Steve Sloan House Manager, Louise Sutton Box Office Supervisor, Jennifer Tallon-Cahill Deputy Chief Electrician, Matthew Taylor Marketing and Press Assistant, Pippa Taylor Press and Media Officer, Marie Thompson Cleaning Supervisor/Receptionist, Scott Turner Market Planning Manager, Hellen Turton Security Officer, Paul Turton Finance Manager, Andy Webster Lighting Technician, Marc Williams Chief Technician (Everyman), Emma Wright Production Manager.

Thanks to all our Front of House team and casual Box Office staff

Board Members:
Cllr Warren Bradley, Professor Michael Brown (Chair), Mike Carran, Michelle Charters, Rod Holmes, Vince Killen, Professor E. Rex Makin, Andrew Moss, Roger Phillips, Sara Williams, Ivan Wadeson.

Company Registration No. 3802476 Registered Charity No. 1081229

The regulations of Liverpool City Council provide that:

The public may leave at the end of the performance by all exit doors and all exit doors must at that time be open. Note: all Liverpool theatres can be emptied in three minutes or less if the audience leaves in an orderly manner.

All gangways, passages, staircases and exits must be kept entirely free from obstruction.

Persons shall not be permitted to stand or sit in any of the intersecting gangways or stand in any unseated space in the auditorium unless standing in such space has been authorised by the City Council.

SMOKING AND DRINKING GLASSES ARE NOT ALLOWED IN THE AUDITORIUM AT ANY TIME.

We would like to remind you that the bleep of digital watches, pagers and mobile phones during the performance may distract the actors and your fellow audience members. Please ensure they are switched off for the duration of the performance. You are strongly advised not to leave bags and other personal belongings unattended anywhere in the theatre.

THE WAY HOME

Chloë Moss

Characters

BOBBY THOMPSON, *sixteen*

PAUL THOMPSON, *thirty-four*

ANGELA THOMPSON, *thirty-three*

DANIEL O'CONNOR, *seventeen, Irish Traveller*

ELLIE O'CONNOR, *eighteen, Irish Traveller*

MARGARET O'DRISCOLL, *forty-one, Irish Traveller*

FELIX O'CONNOR, *forty-five, Irish Traveller*

For the families of Tara Park, Liverpool.

Special thanks to the residents of Tara Park for their warmth and generosity in welcoming me into their homes; Suzanne Bell; Geraldine Judge of Irish Community Care; Tony Glennan; Wynn Lawler; Dawn Taylor; Ken Moss and Patricia Moss. Also to Leanne Best; Claire Cogan; Luke Hayden, Amy McAllister; Nick Moss; Eamonn Owens and Joe Shipman.

This text went to press before the end of rehearsals so may differ slightly from the play as performed

Scene One

Curzon Park, an official Irish travellers' site in Liverpool.
DANIEL *is playing with his football.* ELLIE *is hanging washing
on a circular washing line.* FELIX, *dressed in a sweatshirt
and jeans, is on the steps of the trailer smoking, staring into
the distance.* ELLIE, *wearing a pink crop top and jeans, her
hair up in a high pony, finishes hanging the last of the
washing, as* DANIEL, *wearing a Man United footy top and
tracky bottoms, kicks the ball across it, streaking it with mud.*

ELLIE. Daniel, fer . . . what are yer playin at, yer stupid eejit?

DANIEL. Sorry.

ELLIE. Yer will be.

DANIEL. It was an accident, wan' it?

ELLIE. Accident, me arse.

DANIEL. I swear on –

ELLIE. Yer life. (*Beat.*) Bollocks to yer. Yer'll get struck by
    lightenin' or somethin' one o' these days, I tell yer.

DANIEL. I. Didn't. Fuckin'. Mean it.

ELLIE. Gi' me the ball.

DANIEL. No. (*Beat.*) I'll do the washin' again. I'll hang it out
    an' everythin'.

ELLIE. As if yer will. Jus' gi' me the ball.

DANIEL. What'll yer do wi' it?

ELLIE. Chuck it over the wall.

DANIEL. No way then.

ELLIE. Daniel.

DANIEL. Ah come on, Ellie.

ELLIE. Da, tell him.

Silence.

Da . . . di'yer see that? He's kickin' his shitey ball all over
the washin'.

Silence.

Da.

3

FELIX (*still staring into the distance*). Give her the ball.

DANIEL. Why? It's done now, isn't it? I'm not even bouncin' it or nothin. I'll do the washin' . . . I'll hang it out an' everythin'.

ELLIE. Da.

FELIX. Give yer sister the ball.

DANIEL. Why would I do that on purpose anyway? All's yer gonna do is go mental at me. (*Beat.*) Why would I do it on purpose, eh?

ELLIE. Because yer a little dickhead. Now gi' us the ball.

DANIEL. Jus' so you can throw it over the wall, d'yer think I'm soft?

FELIX. Give it to her.

FELIX *stands and goes inside the trailer.*

DANIEL. It was an accident. How many times –

ELLIE. I don't care what it was. I'm askin' yer to give me that ball before I rip it off yer.

FELIX *walks out of the trailer holding a pair of scissors. He calmly takes the ball from* DANIEL, *stabs it with the scissors, hands it back to him then goes back into the trailer, shutting the door behind him.*

DANIEL. Bastard.

ELLIE. I told yer.

DANIEL. Told me what?

ELLIE. Pushin' it. Yer like a little terrier . . . little fuckin' dog wi' a bone yer are. Never let up.

DANIEL. Bastard.

ELLIE. Sittin' there, face like thunder. I could see that comin', y'know? I told yer. I said give it to me. I said five times give it to me. I was sayin' it fer yer own good.

DANIEL. Oh aye.

ELLIE *takes the muddied washing from the line and dumps it on* DANIEL.

I'm not doin' it now, am I?

ELLIE. Yes yer are . . . yer jus' said.

DANIEL. He burst it on me.

ELLIE. An' he wouldn't a done if yer'd jus' give it to me like I said.

DANIEL *gathers the washing together and sits on the step. He holds the ball in his hands and pushes the air out.* ELLIE *sits next to him.*

Get a new one. S'only a cheapy, eh?

DANIEL. S'not the point.

ELLIE. He's worried, isn' he? (*Beat.*) On edge, like.

DANIEL. An' what are we?

ELLIE. It'll be all right.

DANIEL. Yer can't say that. Yer can't say it'll be all right.

ELLIE. I know it. I've got this feelin' . . . it's gonna be fine.

DANIEL. He's a bastard though, eh?

ELLIE. He's fed up wi' the bickerin', s'all. Yer know wha' he's like. Needs his space. He doesn't let it out, does he? Keeps everythin' all up here. (ELLIE *puts her hand to the top of her chest.*) Like he's been eatin' his tea too fast. (*Pause.*) S'gonna be okay.

Silence.

It will. It'll be . . . all right like.

Offstage a woman's voice can be heard and after a couple of seconds she appears, looking flustered. MARGARET *enters, dressed in jeans and a frilly blouse.*

MARGARET. Jesus Christ Almighty above. Some people. He's a bit of a Hitler, that fella at the gates, isn't he?

ELLIE. Margaret.

MARGARET. I've parked up wi' the caravan an' he's not lettin' me in . . . I've had t'leave it outside on the pavement.

ELLIE. What are yer doin' here?

MARGARET. I'm like, 'Fer Christ sake they're expectin me. Jus' go in and get them if yer don't believe me.' (*Beat.*) Hallo darlin'.

MARGARET *kisses* ELLIE *then* DANIEL.

ELLIE. We wasn't expectin' yer, Margaret.

MARGARET. I left messages.

DANIEL. Margaret, look wha' me da did t'me footy.

ELLIE. Who wi'?

5

MARGARET. I phoned him.

DANIEL. He's a bastard.

ELLIE (*to* MARGARET). Me da?

DANIEL. Margaret –

MARGARET. An' I text him. Coupla times.

DANIEL. Jus' come out an' stabbed the fuckin' thing.

ELLIE. Daniel, shut up, will yer?

MARGARET. Rang him and text him.

ELLIE. He never looks at his phone, Margaret. Sits in the drawer. Switches it off.

MARGARET. He never replied, so I'm thinkin' it's all on, like . . . me comin' t'stay on the site fer a bit.

ELLIE. He switches it off.

MARGARET. What the hell's he bother havin' it for, then?

ELLIE. He doesn't like 'em (*Beat.*) Me mam got him it.

Pause.

MARGARET. S'pose you're workin' yer fingers t'the bone doin' everythin' fer these two?

DANIEL. Eh.

ELLIE. S'all right.

MARGARET. I bet. (*Beat.*) Thought I'd get meself sorted, then get over there.

The door swings open and FELIX *steps out. He is wearing a fluorescent workman's jacket, tar-splattered trousers and heavy boots. He sees* MARGARET, *stops and stares. There's an awkard pause before* MARGARET *speaks.*

Look like yer've seen a ghost.

FELIX. In this case, Margaret, I'm disappointed I haven't.

MARGARET. Charmer.

FELIX. What d'yer want?

MARGARET. Did yer not get me messages?

ELLIE. Margaret called yer, Da . . . left yer a message.

MARGARET. And I texted. Texted yer a coupla' messages.

FELIX. Sayin' what, exactly?

MARGARET. Yer didn't get me messages?

FELIX *gets the phone from the drawer. He switches it on, listens to the messages, turns it off and puts it back in the drawer.*

Well?

FELIX. No. Yer can't.

ELLIE. Da!

MARGARET. Aah Felix, c'mon.

FELIX. Come on nothin'.

MARGARET. This isn't what Winnie'd want –

FELIX. Don't bring me wife's name into this, Margaret.

MARGARET. Aah shut up, will yer? It isn't what she'll be wanting now, is it? I want t'help out –

FELIX. We don't need any help.

MARGARET. Looks like it.

FELIX. Yer'll have t'go.

Pause.

MARGARET. We're all of us in the same boat.

FELIX. How's that, then?

MARGARET. Me sister's in hospital, for cryin' out loud. I wanna see her.

FELIX. Why? Yer never see her when she's out a' hospital.

MARGARET. An' who's t'blame for that?

FELIX. Not me.

MARGARET. It wouldn't be, no. Wouldn't be nothin' t'do wi' you.

FELIX *walks slowly towards* MARGARET.

FELIX. It wouldn't be. No.

They stand staring at each other for a few moments.

MARGARET. Well, I'm here now.

FELIX. Pity it's a wasted trip then, isn't it?

ELLIE. Da . . . will yer jus' –

FELIX. Yer not stoppin' here.

MARGARET. An' how yer gonna stop me, Felix? Own the whole friggin' site, do yer? There's space between your trailer and next door's.

FELIX. You have t'be here as my guest.

MARGARET. An' here I am.

FELIX. Yer not my guest.

Pause.

MARGARET. I rang the hospital before. Yer haven't been since the day before yesterday. She's makin' excuses for yer, as usual. Givin' it all, 'Aah, he's workin' so hard, it must be a strain.'

FELIX. She'll be out in a few days.

MARGARET. Yer her husband.

FELIX. Are you tryin' a make me get angry, Margaret?

ELLIE. Aah, come on, please . . . there's no need for all this, is there?

MARGARET. I'm not tryin' a' *make* yer do anythin'.

ELLIE. Da, jus' for a little bit, yeah?

FELIX. No.

MARGARET. Aah now, why yer bein' like this? So I said a few little things, about a million years ago –

BOBBY *slowly enters on a bike. He is wearing a school uniform and holding a football under one arm. He gets off the bike, lays it on the floor and walks cautiously towards* DANIEL, ELLIE, FELIX *and* MARGARET.

FELIX. One o' them that sticks in me head bein', 'Wha' in the name of Jesus are yer doin' with that useless bastard, he's not fit fer firewood.'

MARGARET. Your problem, Felix, is that you've too good a memory. (*Beat.*) It's all in the past for me.

FELIX. Aye, an' you're all in the past for me.

DANIEL *notices* BOBBY. *He doesn't acknowledge his presence.*

BOBBY. All right. (*He bounces the ball and drops it. It rolls under the trailer. He lets it go.*) Daniel?

DANIEL. Yeah.

BOBBY. All right.

Silence.

It's Bobby.

DANIEL. I know.

8

MARGARET. If yer want me gone, Felix, yer gonna have to physically move me yerself.

BOBBY. Fancy a game?

DANIEL. No.

BOBBY. Wha' happened to yer ball?

FELIX. If yer not gone by the time I get back, Margaret – I will . . . Daniel, get yer gear on, we're late.

DANIEL. I left me jacket at Patrick an' Kathleen's.

FELIX. Well, shift yer arse an' get it, then.

BOBBY. Yer goin' out?

DANIEL *ignores* BOBBY. *He walks off in the direction of the other trailers.* BOBBY *stands, looking at* ELLIE.

ELLIE. What?

BOBBY. Nothin'.

FELIX. Can I help yer, son?

BOBBY. I jus' . . . I was jus' seein' if Dan fancied a game.

FELIX. His name's Daniel an' he's goin' to work. (*Beat.*) Goodbye, Margaret.

MARGARET. See yer in a bit.

FELIX. Goodbye, I said.

MARGARET. See yers later.

FELIX. Goodbye.

ELLIE. Oh, for Jaysus' sake.

FELIX. Tell him I'll be waitin' in the van.

FELIX *walks away.*

BOBBY. I'm Bobby.

MARGARET. Fuckin' good for you.

MARGARET *exits in the same direction as* FELIX. BOBBY *stands for a second or two, shifting about awkwardly.*

BOBBY. Could I get me ball back, please?

ELLIE *gestures to go ahead and watches as* BOBBY *starts to peer under the caravan. He stares intently, crouched down, his hands on his knees.*

I can't see it. (*Pause.*) Must have rolled right in the middle or something. (*Pause.*) Have yer got a stick?

9

ELLIE. No.

BOBBY. It's dark. (*He lies flat, his cheek pressed against the floor.*) I think . . . I reckon I might be able to see it. Can I go under?

ELLIE. Go for yer life.

BOBBY *disappears underneath the trailer, wiggling along on his stomach. ELLIE goes over and peers underneath. From around the other side comes DANIEL, wearing a fluorescent work jacket. He is bouncing BOBBY's football.*

BOBBY (*to ELLIE, from under the trailer still*). Nah . . . it's a doll's head.

DANIEL *heads the ball in the air, catches it, and exits. ELLIE stands and goes back inside.*

Scene Two

PAUL *and* ANG's *kitchen.* PAUL *is standing at the window.* ANG *sits at the table putting make-up on.*

PAUL. Ah eh, that's takin' the piss that is.

ANG. What are yer on about?

PAUL. There's *two* caravans parked up on the street there, Angela. Two.

ANG. So?

PAUL. So they've got a campsite to live in. (*Beat.*) They're spreadin' out. It's like fuckin' Billy Smart's circus out there. Where's the phone book? I'm ringin' the council again.

ANG. What d'yer need the phone book for? Should have it on speed dial.

PAUL. Yer don't get more live an' let live than me but that's fuckin' ridiculous. Be sittin' on the window ledge next.

ANG. Paul, yer can hardly even see them. Might not be Gyppo's anyway.

PAUL. Yeah, coz it's a lovely holiday spot that, isn't it? Can't exactly imagine a family o' four bailin' out with their buckets an' spades. (*Beat.*) Have yer locked that shed?

ANG. Yeah, an' I've got a load o' tins in as well. (*Beat.*) Gonna stick the tape on the windows later n'all.

PAUL. Yer can laugh, Angela.

ANG. If only.

PAUL. What's it doin' to the value of this place, eh? Seriously, who's gonna wanna buy a house opposite a fuckin' Gyppo site?

ANG. Yer've gotta get on a chair and stretch yer neck by about a foot to even know it's there. Look at the height of that wall? It's like Alcatraz.

ANG sits back down and continues putting her make-up on. PAUL picks a leaflet up from the countertop.

PAUL. An' have yer got onto this?

ANG. What?

PAUL. This.

He passes the leaflet to ANG.

Thee can't even spell.

ANG. What am I lookin' at?

PAUL points to a word on the leaflet.

That is how yer spell 'tarmac'.

PAUL looks at the leaflet again, then rips it up and puts it in the bin.

PAUL. I'll give them fuckin' tarmac. S'outrageous.

ANG. Why?

PAUL. What d'yer mean 'why'?

ANG. What's so outrageous about someone tryin' to make a livin'? What's the difference between you doin' yer bits an' bobs on the side an' them doin' their thing?

PAUL. Because they're rippin' people off, Angela. I don't rip people off. Bit o' moonlightin' at weekends, paintin' and decoratin', sortin' out people's gardens for a decent price an' doin' a good job isn't ripping people off. It's all a big con. They're thieves.

ANG. How do you know that?

PAUL. Two sets of ladders, a Henri Lloyd jacket, a box o' knock off adidas bags from the shed and our fuckin' cat goin' missin' is how I know that –

ANG. For Christ's sake, Paul. Fluffy died.

PAUL. Where's his body then?

ANG. He would've dragged himself off somewhere. Thee know, cats, when they're gonna die. It's what thee do.

PAUL. It's what thievin' Gyppos do.

ANG. Paul, yer couldn't've given him away. He had a tumour the size of a footy in his belly. He was blind an' he fuckin' stunk to high hell. He wasn't exactly an advert for Whiskas. (*Beat.*) An' yer were asking for it with those ladders, leavin' them in the entry. The window cleaner probably had them off.

PAUL. Come off it.

ANG. Put yer energy into somethin' else . . . somethin' useful. (*Beat.*) Somethin' positive.

PAUL. Oh fuckin' hell, Ang . . . don't start goin' into one, depressin' me. Please. It's Friday night.

ANG. I'm not 'goin' into one'. How's that 'goin' into one'? I'm just sayin' . . .

PAUL. Well don't. Not now.

ANG. Why not?

PAUL. Coz we're goin' out.

ANG. So? (*Beat.*) I can't say how I feel just coz we're goin' out?

PAUL. PMT time, is it?

ANG (*staring at* PAUL). Unfortunately it probably is, yeah.

PAUL. Sorry. (*Beat.*) I didn't think.

ANG. You never do.

PAUL. We can go an' see someone again. Get it looked at.

ANG. 'It.'

PAUL. Bit of a once-over.

ANG. I'm not a Ford Escort.

PAUL. Sorry, I didn't mean it to come out like that. I just think it's the sensible thing to do.

ANG. Sensible sounds all funny when you say it, Paul.

PAUL. Make an appointment.

ANG. They'll say the same thing. We've been through it all. There's nothing wrong. It's probably us, we're a bad combination.

PAUL. We've done it once before. Got the evidence, face trippin' him twenty-four hours a day to prove it.

ANG. Sixteen years ago. (*Beat.*) A lot can happen in sixteen years.

12

PAUL. It'll be okay. Come 'ere.

He puts his arms around ANG.

Come on, babe. We'll talk about it later, yeah?

ANG. Paul, I wish you were as laid-back about everything else . . . yer son's a depressive agoraphobic with no friends an' yer can't have more kids but that's like water off a duck's back. That'll look after itself, no sweat. Stick a couple o' caravans outside the window an' all hell breaks loose. Is this all there is? Eh . . . Paul, is this it?

PAUL. Ah Angela, come on, I wanna relax. I don't wanna start havin' one o' them fuckin' . . . talks. (*Beat.*) Spins me head out.

ANG. Here y'are, that's exactly what I mean. (*Pause.*) I remember when you used to wake me up in the middle of the night to talk . . . about anythin' and everythin' . . . the size of the sky an' what it all means –

PAUL. That was weed.

ANG. No it wasn't, Paul. That was before yer give up on things. When practically everythin' was still possible.

PAUL. See, this is what I mean, Ang. Yer givin' me palpitations.

ANG. You made me promise that when Bobby was old enough we'd take him off round the world, that it didn't matter that we were kids with a baby. We'd go travellin' . . . go to India. Just fuck off somewhere.

PAUL. An' you said yer didn't wanna coz it'd be irresponsible and he'd probably get Malaria and die.

ANG. I know. (*Beat.*) I'm sorry.

PAUL. Don't be sorry – you were right. It was a stupid idea.

ANG. I wish we had.

PAUL. Takin' a toddler round the world . . . comin' back to nothin'. We wouldn't've been able to get a house if we had.

ANG. So what? I mean, honestly, why was that such a big deal, eh? Owning a house at twenty. Half my mates are still renting now an' they don't care . . . what's the big accomplishment about havin' a mortgage round yer neck? 'Owning' somewhere. (*Beat.*) So what – that we can knock the front room through an' stick a conservatory on the kitchen? Fuckin' whoopee.

PAUL. Right. Nice one.

ANG. In fact, I can't even remember havin' a conversation about it . . . it was just, 'I've been the estate agent, here's a photey, can we use yer dad's van?'

PAUL. So what was all that about it bein' 'the most amazin' thing anyone's ever done for yer'?

ANG. It was – I'm not –

PAUL. So I work me knackers off. Get us some security. A house. Things.

ANG. I'm not interested in 'things'.

PAUL. Bollocks. (*Beat.*) Been to yoga, have yer? I'd like to hear yer say yer not interested in things when we're in Lewis's tomorrow.

ANG. I'm talkin' on a deeper level.

PAUL. Deep, me arsehole. I did what I thought was right, what I thought was 'positive' –

ANG. Oh, I'm sorry for ruining yer fuckin' life, Paul.

PAUL. I'm not sayin' that, Angela. Positive, I said . . . as in good. As in what I wanted. I can't do right for doing wrong round 'ere.

ANG. I'm just expressin' thought, Paul. (*Beat.*) It's what yer do unless yer a complete potato-head that sits in front o' the telly watchin' Jeremy Kyle and readin' the fuckin' *Mirror* every day. (*Pause.*) I wanna feel hopeful. I haven't for ages. Years. I'm young. That's the best thing about being young. Hope. I wanna look out the window an' see a sunny day. (*Beat.*) 'Things' don't make me happy, Paul.

PAUL. Don't thee, no?

PAUL *picks up* ANG*'s make-up bag and tips it out onto the table.*

Yer spend a fuckin' shitload of money on staying miserable then.

ANG. Just because I wear Clinique lippy doesn't mean that I haven't got a fucking imagination, yer stupid twat.

The door opens and BOBBY *enters in his school uniform.*

BOBBY. What's goin' on?

ANG. Nothin' . . . hi, babe.

BOBBY. Noisy nothin'.

PAUL. Bob, go upstairs an' pack a suitcase.

BOBBY. What for?

PAUL. We're goin' to India.

BOBBY. Yer messin'?

PAUL. No.

BOBBY. India? As in the country?

PAUL. Yeah. Go on. Get yer snorkel out the loft.

BOBBY. Yer bein' serious?

ANG. Bobby –

BOBBY. How long for?

PAUL. Forever.

BOBBY. Honestly?

PAUL. Yeah.

BOBBY. We're movin' to India?

PAUL. We are moving to India.

ANG. Bobby, take no notice. He's bein' a dickhead.

PAUL. No I'm not.

BOBBY. What about school?

PAUL. We'll get yer a job. Pullin' a rickshaw or somethin'.

ANG. We're not goin' to India, Bobby.

    Pause.

BOBBY. Dad . . . are we?

    PAUL *sits down at the table, puts his head in his hands.*

PAUL. No. We're not.

BOBBY. Oh, I hate yer . . . why d'yer say things like that
    when yer not serious? It's not fair.

PAUL. I'm just tryin' a' please everyone, mate. Apparently yer
    mum's pissed off that I worked hard an' got us a house
    instead of pissin' it all up the wall and draggin' yer both
    half way round the world on a student loan.

BOBBY. I well would've rather done that.

PAUL. Thanks for yer support, son.

ANG. Paul, will yer stop involvin' him in our arguments?

BOBBY. It would've been boss, that.

15

PAUL. Sound. Well, I tell yer what, why don't you two plan yer fuckin' escape route while I go an' have a pint.

PAUL stands and puts his jacket on.

I'll show yer a sunny day, Angela. Come to work with me. (*Beat.*) I sit in a box for ten hours at a time an' watch sunny days go past so you've got a fuckin' window to look out of.

ANG. An' what do I do like? Swan round all day paintin' me nails? I paid for those windows n'all.

PAUL. Keep yer money. I don't want yer money. (*Beat.*) Save up. Get yerself a plane ticket.

ANG. Oh Paul, come on, don't be an arsehole.

PAUL. Angela. (*Beat.*) Can yer please stop callin' me things?

He walks out and slams the door shut.

ANG. Prick.

BOBBY sits down next to his mum.

BOBBY. Everythin's about money in this house.

ANG. Everythin's about money everywhere.

Scene Three

Curzon Park. Inside the trailer. It is crammed with crockery and ornaments but is ordered and tidy. The upholstery and curtains are a rich red and the seating is covered in clear plastic to keep it clean. Large gilt-framed pictures of family hang on the walls. MARGARET and ELLIE enter. MARGARET takes off her coat and switches the kettle on. ELLIE, still wearing her coat, sits on the couch.

ELLIE. I hate them places.

Silence.

Margaret, I hate them places.

MARGARET. I know. But it's the best place t'be, y'know? They're where people get better.

ELLIE. They're where people die.

MARGARET. Don't be talkin' rubbish like that. (*Pause.*) She's not gonna die.

ELLIE. She will in the end.

MARGARET. We all will in the end.

ELLIE. She looks so thin.

MARGARET. I think she's lookin' okay. There's pink in her cheeks, y'know . . . definitely pickin' up a bit.

ELLIE. I'm not a kid. Yer don't have to pretend.

MARGARET. I'm not pretendin' nothin'. You need t'stop yerself gettin' carried away you do. She needs a rest an' she's gettin' one. She's all right. Yer heard what thee said. Out this time next week if she carries on the way she's goin'.

The kettle boils. MARGARET *pours the tea and brings it through to* ELLIE. *She hands her a cup and sits down beside her.*

Yer not stoppin'?

ELLIE *takes off her coat.*

ELLIE. I jus' don't trust them.

MARGARET. Who?

ELLIE. Doctors. Doesn't feel like they're tellin' the truth.

MARGARET. An' what are thee gonna go and lie t'yer for?

ELLIE. Jus' wanna get yer out o' their faces. 'Oh, she's doin' grand, pardon me but I gotta run.'

MARGARET. They can't lie. They're not allowed.

ELLIE. I can do that, what they're doin'. Them nurses. Gi' us the stuff an' I can do it here. At home. People get forgotten about in places like that. Wait two hours fer a glass o' water.

MARGARET. She's not waitin for nothin', she's bein' looked after.

ELLIE. Why can't we jus' look after her at home?

MARGARET. We can. Next week when thee see fit t'let her out. Until then we can go in an' see her every day.

ELLIE. A poxy hour. Go an' get a cuppa an' come back an' it's time t'leave. (*Beat.*) That old fat nurse wi' her clipboard wavin' it round, practically stickin' it in me face. I thought, 'Get it any closer, love, and you'll need fuckin' surgery yourself t'remove it'.

Silence.

MARGARET. Has yer da mentioned goin' in anytime this week?

Silence.

I think it's disgustin' . . . wha' the hell's up wi' him?

17

ELLIE. He doesn't like hospitals.

MARGARET. Isn't that just unique? Y'know I love 'em meself, like. Sometimes I go in wi'a great big bag o' grapes an' a bottle o' lucozade and just wander up an' down the wards, crackin' on like I'm visitin' someone. Doesn't like hospitals, who does? (*Beat.*) Wha' does he think he's playin' at, eh?

ELLIE. Got a ting, hasn't he? Superstition like.

MARGARET. Ah well, bollocks to him . . . I can't be doin' with excuses. Yer put thee effort in however yer feelin'. Yer do it fer yer family.

ELLIE. Aye. (*Beat.*) Thanks Margaret. Fer comin', like.

MARGARET. Ah, shurrup.

ELLIE. Tings all right in Kent, like?

MARGARET. Grand. Fine. Grand. (*Beat.*) Been on the road a bit though this las' month . . . jus' fancied a change o'scenery, like.

ELLIE. Weather's gettin' nice.

MARGARET. Was in Cork las' weekend fer Mary Ann's weddin'.

ELLIE. Mary Ann? To who?

MARGARET. Some dopey lookin' eejit. (*Beat.*) Kathleen's cousin's son. She's only jus' turned sixteen. Don't you be gettin' no funny ideas about tha' sort o thing. Too young by a mile.

ELLIE. As if.

MARGARET. Went on the boat. Threw up the whole way there. Then got some God-forsaken B&B for me trouble. Made us get up an' out at six.

ELLIE. Six o'clock? In the mornin'?

MARGARET. Shoulda jus' had a sign there on the door sayin' 'No Travellers'. Ummin and ahhing they was an' I'm practically beggin' . . . practically on the floor. Palms together. Face t' the sky.

ELLIE. Yer get any breakfast made?

MARGARET. Continental.

ELLIE. Continental?

MARGARET. Jam on toast.

ELLIE. Jam on fuckin' toast and out by six? How much?

MARGARET. Seventy euros.

ELLIE. Cheeky bastards.

MARGARET. To tell the truth I wouldn't have wanted fried anyway. Not that early in the mornin'.

ELLIE. No. (*Beat.*) Bet yer were glad t'get home, eh?

Pause. MARGARET *comes and sits down next to* ELLIE.

MARGARET. Listen . . . I had somethin' I wanted t'talk t'yer about. About Home like. Kent.

The door opens and DANIEL *enters, closely followed by* FELIX. *They are wearing their work gear. They kick their boots off and leave them by the door.*

The workers return.

FELIX *ignores her and goes into the bedroom.* DANIEL *sits on the couch.* ELLIE *stands and picks up both pairs of boots. She puts them into a carrier bag.*

DANIEL. How's me mam, did yer see her?

ELLIE. Daniel, get that shitty thing off yer back before yer go sittin' down spreadin' muck everywhere.

DANIEL *takes the jacket off hurriedly.*

DANIEL. Is she all right or what?

MARGARET. She's grand, son . . . grand.

DANIEL. Did yers tell her I'm comin' in tomorrer like?

MARGARET. Course we did.

FELIX *comes out of the bedroom.*

She sends her love. Can't wait to see yer. World o' good it did her us goin' in today. Really perked her up. Very important gettin' yer visits when yer stuck in a hospital bed.

FELIX *gets a mug from the cupboard and slams it down on the counter. He flicks the kettle on.*

FELIX. We're gonna have t' get out earlier in the mornin', Daniel.

DANIEL. Earlier than seven o'clock?

FELIX. Make up fer wasted time today. Make up fer all your piss-arsin' around . . . think yer were some little babby the way yer workin' lately.

MARGARET. Maybe he's got things on his mind.

19

FELIX. Maybe it's got fuck all to do wi' you.

ELLIE. Da –

MARGARET. Ellie, don't bother, love. S'like water off a duck's back.

FELIX. I mean it, son, yer gonna have to buck yer ideas up sharpish. I'm doin' the work o' two men here.

MARGARET. Give yerself a break then. (*Beat.*) Go an' sit wi' yer wife fer a bit.

FELIX steps toward MARGARET, then stops. He stares at her for a few seconds.

FELIX. I'm goin' out now, Margaret. I can't stop yer bein' here but I can stop yer from parkin' yer fat arse on my settee mornin', noon and night. Yer've got a caravan ten foot away and I'd be grateful if yer were in it when I got back.

Silence. FELIX starts thumping around the trailer.

Ellie, what did yer do wi' me boots?

ELLIE. Put them in tha' bag.

FELIX. Can't put somethin' down fer two seconds round here without someone packin' it away.

ELLIE. I was gonna clean them.

FELIX gets the boots out of the bag and puts them on again. He stands and picks up a stack of leaflets from the side.

FELIX. Would yer look over this fer us?

ELLIE takes the leaflet and studies it before handing it back to FELIX.

ELLIE. Fine.

FELIX. No mistakes?

ELLIE. No.

FELIX takes the leaflet back.

Thank you, Ellie.

FELIX. Out at six tomorrer. Need t'get a good eight hours in –

DANIEL. Six o'clock? Yer takin' the piss, yeah?

FELIX. Need t'make up lost time, sunshine, so unless yer wanna work all weekend n'all –

DANIEL. I'm not workin' all weekend, Da.

FELIX. Then six o'clock an' shut up about it.

DANIEL. Can't we get someone else? Paddy'll help out or somethin', eh?

FELIX. Can't afford it . . . jus', if yer jus' pulled yer finger out.

MARGARET. Leave him alone will yer, Felix, fer Christ's sake.

FELIX. Margaret, I'm warnin' yer –

There is a knock on the trailer door, ELLIE *opens it and* BOBBY *steps in.* FELIX *disappears into the bedroom.*

MARGARET. Hello son, come in.

BOBBY *stays standing nervously in the doorway.*

Come on, come in . . .

BOBBY *enters.*

Sit down . . . d'yer wanna cuppa?

BOBBY. Erm, no, thanks very much. (*Beat. To* DANIEL.) All right?

Silence.

D'yer wanna game?

DANIEL. No.

ELLIE. Don't be so rude t'the lad, Daniel.

DANIEL. I don't feel like it.

MARGARET. Bit of a kick around. Bit o' fresh air . . . do yer the world o' good.

BOBBY. Yer don't 'ave to like.

DANIEL. I know. I'm not goin' to.

BOBBY. Can I 'ave me footy back then?

Pause. DANIEL *goes into his room and gets the football. He steps outside the trailer.* BOBBY *follows.* DANIEL *starts to do keep ups and* BOBBY *sits on the floor watching him.*

DANIEL. Yer not go to school?

BOBBY. Nah. Fucked it off. Don't go in no more.

DANIEL. Where d'yer go?

BOBBY *shrugs. Silence.*

BOBBY. Went to town this mornin'. Pictures. (*Beat.*) Some . . . foreign film at the place wi' the cafe an' bar an' that.

French. It had subtitles. It was about this brother and sister, right, and they end up getting off wi' each other. (*Beat.*) It was weird, man.

DANIEL (*still has the ball, but his interest has been caught*). Yeah?

BOBBY. I fell asleep for a bit in the middle, and it didn't make much sense when I woke up. I think I missed somethin'. (*Beat.*) You're so boss at that.

Silence.

Then I went the Albert Dock. (*Beat.*) It's so shit, the Albert Dock, isn't it?

DANIEL. Dunno.

BOBBY. Haven't yer been the Albert Dock?

DANIEL. Yeah. Once. Thought it was all right. Didn't think it was shite, didn't think it was fuckin' great either. Thought it was all right.

BOBBY. Yeah, it's all right I s'pose. It was better when Richard and Judy were there. (*Beat.*) I was on Richard and Judy once, yer know?

DANIEL. Doin' what?

BOBBY. Yer could just see me like. Through the window behind them. I stayed for the whole programme though and they waved at me.

DANIEL. But yer weren't actually on it?

Silence.

BOBBY. Where yer from?

DANIEL. Here.

BOBBY. Liverpool?

DANIEL. Here.

BOBBY. Yer speak . . . Irish, isn't it? Yer accent like. Whereabouts?

DANIEL. I was born here.

BOBBY. Were yer?

DANIEL *nods.*

I thought Gypsies travelled about like.

DANIEL. I'm a Traveller.

BOBBY. But yer not though, are yer? If yer don't actually travel anywhere.

DANIEL. What d'you know?

BOBBY. Nothin'. I wasn't bein' funny.

DANIEL. Yer don't know nothin' about it.

BOBBY. I know. (*Long pause.*) What's it like? In there like. Livin' there an' that?

DANIEL *shrugs*.

Me nan lives in a bungalow.

Pause.

I like not havin' to go up the stairs. They're crap, stairs, aren't they?

Silence.

I had this mad dream last night about stairs. (*Pause.*) D'yer ever have end o' the world dreams?

DANIEL. Eh?

BOBBY. Dreams where it's the end of the world? I have them all the time. Different . . . scenarios like. (*Beat.*) Last night it was happening again. (*Beat.*) There was an earthquake, right? An' the only way yer could get saved was by leggin' up all these millions of stairs in this weird sorta buildin'. Like a tower or something. (*Beat.*) At the top was this roof, yeah? If yer made it onto the roof then yer were all right. (*Pause.*) I made it and I was well chuffed obviously, but then, I realised that the rest of the world didn't exist anymore coz it had been destroyed an' I didn't have any food or water so I'd just have to starve to death by meself on the roof.

Silence.

Otterspool's good, y'know? I like goin' there . . . along the prom. Go most days on me bike. Gonna go tomorrow. Take the footy if yer wanna come?

DANIEL. Workin'.

BOBBY. Where d'yer work?

DANIEL. Help me da.

BOBBY. Doin' what?

DANIEL. Graftin'. (*Beat.*) Pavin', roofin', tarmaccing . . . hard stuff, makes yer sweat from yer eyebrows.

BOBBY. My dad's a security guard. Just sits there. An' he's got this sorta DIY business that he does on weekends an' that. But he's rubbish really. Should see our house, everythin's wonky.

Silence.

Yer ma and da argue loads, don't thee? Mine are like that.

DANIEL. She's me aunty. Me mam's in hospital.

BOBBY. Sorry.

Silence. DANIEL drops the ball.

What's yer record?

DANIEL. Two thousand and fifty-three.

BOBBY. Fuck off.

DANIEL doesn't respond, he just sits on the step of the trailer, holding the ball.

That's loads.

DANIEL turns and walks into the trailer. BOBBY stands and follows. MARGARET eyes him.

MARGARET. Smart uniform. (*To* DANIEL.) It's a shame yer didn't stay on, son. Do yer exams.

FELIX. It's a shame he got seven shades o' shite knocked out of him.

MARGARET. There's other schools.

FELIX. There's other bullies.

DANIEL. He doesn't go either. Just pretends to his ma and da he does.

MARGARET. How much longer yer gotta keep that up for?

BOBBY. Not long. Exams soon, then I'm finished.

MARGARET. They're tough them pretend exams, aren't thee?

DANIEL. Better than workin' yer fingers t' the bone every day.

FELIX. How would you know about workin' yer fingers to the bone? We're three days behind on this job coz yer doin' the exact opposite t' workin yer fingers to the bone.

DANIEL. We need another pair o' hands.

FELIX. We just need you to pull yer finger out, s'all we need.

DANIEL. Da, tha's bollocks, there's no way –

MARGARET. Get one of Paddy's lot to gi' yer a hand.

FELIX. They've all got jobs on. I went over yesterday. (*Pause.*)
An' this is the same fella I took practically a fortnight
convincin' him that we'd get it done within a week an' it'd
all be grand an' he's givin' me all this chat about gettin'
someone 'proper' like I'm a fuckin' tailor's dummy an'
I feel like tellin' him t'shove it but I can't coz I need the
money so I'm givin' him a rock bottom price an' almost
offerin' a week's work for nothin', until he –

BOBBY. I'll help yer.

FELIX. What?

BOBBY. I'll help yer out. If yer need someone fer a couple o'
days.

DANIEL. Yer don't know anythin' about it.

BOBBY. Yer can show us . . . I'll do the crap bits.

DANIEL. It's all crap bits.

BOBBY. I don't mind.

FELIX. Have yer done any o' this sort a thing before?

BOBBY. Not much. Not really. (*Beat.*) No.

FELIX. There's some stuff yer could do, I suppose. I'd pay yer
the goin' rate.

BOBBY. I'm not bothered about gettin' paid. Could be like
work experience or somethin'.

FELIX. I'm no crook. (*Beat.*) Fifteen quid a day.

BOBBY. Sound.

FELIX. Jus' fer a few days. Start tomorrow if yer like.

BOBBY. Okay, yeah.

FELIX. On a trial basis like. See how yer get on in the
mornin'.

BOBBY. I'm a good worker. Helped me dad do our extension.

DANIEL. What . . . holdin' stuff for him?

BOBBY. Not just that. I used the drill as well.

FELIX. Yer won't be needin' to use a drill but there's probably
a fair bit o' holdin stuff yer can do.

DANIEL. Da, we'll be all right.

BOBBY. I'm good at a few things. Do I need to wear anything
special, Mr O'Connor?

FELIX. D'yer have a reflective panelled Donkey jacket?

BOBBY. No.

FELIX. Steel-capped boots?

BOBBY. No.

FELIX. Overalls?

BOBBY. No.

FELIX. Hard hat?

Pause.

BOBBY. I've got a cycling helmet.

FELIX. Stick yer cycling hat on and a pair o' old jeans then. Be grand. (*He grabs the leaflets and goes to leave.*) Eight o'clock then. Sharp.

FELIX *leaves.* DANIEL *stares at* BOBBY *who is beaming.*

BOBBY. It'll be boss that, won't it?

DANIEL *stands.*

Where yer goin'? See yer tomorrer then, yeah?

Silence. DANIEL *leaves.*

Scene Four

The kitchen. PAUL *is going back and forth to the yard. There is a toolbox on the table.* BOBBY *sits.*

PAUL. So what d'yer reckon?

BOBBY. The Zutons?

PAUL. Yeah.

BOBBY. A band?

PAUL. No flies on you mate, is thee?

BOBBY. Me an' you?

PAUL. Yeah. We can go an' see them and then go out after somewhere.

BOBBY. Where?

PAUL. Heebiejeebies. Wherever.

Silence.

BOBBY. Why?

PAUL. What d'yer mean, why? (*Beat.*) For fun.

BOBBY. I won't get in.

PAUL. Yeah, yer will. Yer'll be wi' me, won't yer?

Silence.

BOBBY. I don't wanna.

PAUL. You'll get in, stop flappin'.

BOBBY. I'm not . . . I just don't wanna.

PAUL. See the Zutons, or see the Zutons with me?

BOBBY. Both.

Silence.

Sorry.

PAUL. Doesn't matter.

BOBBY. Have I hurt yer feelin's?

PAUL. Shurrup.

BOBBY. I 'ave. I'm not into them.

PAUL. How d'yer know if yer've never listened to them?

BOBBY. I'm jus' not into goin' to see bands.

PAUL. All right. Forget it then, eh?

Silence.

Do somethin' else instead.

BOBBY. What like?

PAUL. Whatever. Anythin' . . . what d'yer wanna do?

Pause.

BOBBY. Nothin'.

PAUL. We'll do nothin' then, eh?

BOBBY. I'm okay, yer know.

PAUL. I know, I'm just . . .

BOBBY. What?

PAUL. Tryin'.

BOBBY. Then . . . don't.

PAUL *stops what he's doing.*

I don't mean . . . I mean yer shouldn't have to try. (*Beat.*) Just act naturally.

PAUL. Act naturally?

BOBBY. Stop forcin' things.

PAUL. Fuckin' hell, mate . . . I'm askin' me son if he wants to come out into town wi' me. Yer makin' me feel like some sort of –

BOBBY. I know . . . I know you mean well, like.

PAUL. Yer know I mean well? Bobby, I'm yer dad.

BOBBY. Exactly. (*Beat.*) I don't wanna go an' watch a band with you an' yer mates. I'm just . . . thanks, like. I'm all right, y'know.

PAUL. I know yer are.

Silence.

Tommo's little brother's comin'.

BOBBY. So?

PAUL. He's only eighteen. He's boss, yer know.

BOBBY. He's a knobhead.

PAUL. No, he isn't.

BOBBY. I've seen him around. He walks like that.

BOBBY *does an exaggerated swagger.*

PAUL. Coz he goes the gym loads, doesn't he? Boxes.

BOBBY. Yer want him to teach me how t'fight? Turn me into a sted head?

PAUL. No . . . he's not like that, anyway.

BOBBY. Tell that to the lad he put in Fazakerley.

PAUL. Self-defence.

BOBBY. Oh aye, yeah.

Silence.

PAUL. Who was that lad last year?

BOBBY. I dunno.

PAUL. Little fella. Used to knock most days. 'Hello Mr Thompson, is Wobert in?' Couldn't say his 'R's'.

BOBBY. Can't remember.

PAUL. Yes yer can, it's not like yer had them queuin', mate. He was the only one, how've yer forgotten him?

BOBBY. David Robinson.

PAUL. David, that's it. Always gettin' one of us to say you were out . . . he was all right, him.

BOBBY. He was a whopper. He played with figures of gnomes.

PAUL. He wanted to be yer friend.

BOBBY. An' what? I'm meant to be grateful?

PAUL. I'm just sayin'. I'm sayin' just . . . give things a chance.

Pause.

Thanks for helpin'.

BOBBY. S'all right.

PAUL *goes outside and into the shed. He comes out
wearing a fabric toolbelt – the sort that looks a bit like an
apron.*

Wha' are yer wearin' an apron for?

PAUL. It's fer me tools, soft lad. Gotta look the part, haven't
yer? Gonna start floodin' in soon . . . got me ad in the *Echo*
on Monday.

BOBBY. Why d'yer need another job, anway?

PAUL. To keep yer mother in the lifestyle she's become
accustomed to.

BOBBY. What's the point in working all week and weekends?
That's depressin', that.

PAUL. It's life, mate.

BOBBY. It's not like we're poor.

PAUL. How d'you know?

BOBBY. Coz we're not.

PAUL. Yer won't be complaining when yer flyin' out somewhere
boss in the summer, will yer? After yer exams, lyin' on a
beach.

Silence.

Come out wi' me if yer like . . . on a job. Giz a hand.

BOBBY. I'm all right.

PAUL. Pay yer.

BOBBY. Nah.

PAUL. Go on.

Pause.

BOBBY. I've got a job.

PAUL. Yer what?

BOBBY. After school. Paper round.

PAUL. Bit old fer that, aren't yer?

BOBBY. Just till after me exams.

PAUL. Shit money.

BOBBY. Don't need any money.

PAUL. Yer'll grow outa that.

BOBBY. Money is the root of all evil.

ANG *enters. She is struggling with shopping bags. She puts a couple down on the floor then goes back out, returning a few seconds later with more.*

ANG. No, honest, I'm fine. I need the exercise.

BOBBY *goes outside, picks up some bags and starts carrying them through to the kitchen.*

Ta, love.

BOBBY *exits.* ANG *plants a kiss on* PAUL's *cheek. He barely responds.*

All right, Angela, how's it goin', love?

PAUL. All right, Angela, hows it goin', love?

ANG. What's up with you?

PAUL. Marty Carr, yeah, picks his lad up every third weekend. (*Beat.*) If he can be arsed. (*Pause.*) They sit in his flat while Marty smokes weed an' the kid reads *The Match*. Then he gives him a quid an' drops him off the next day before the pub opens. I bumped into them last week in the street. Started talkin' about goin' for a bevvie at the weekend and Marty starts givin' it all this, 'got lumbered with Alfie so I can't come' an' the kid's lookin' at him like he's God. Face beamin'.

Pause.

ANG. Yer've got a cob on coz Marty Carr doesn't spend enough time with his son?

PAUL. I've got a cob on because I try to be the best father that I can, an' what's the point?

ANG. What's the point in bein' a good dad?

PAUL. It doesn't get me anywhere, does it? I feel like I'm being punished. 'Money is the root of all evil' . . . I'd like to hear him say that next time I'm buying him allsorts o' shite.

ANG. Stop buyin' him allsorts o' shite then. Fuckin' 'ell, Paul.

PAUL. I just wanna make things easier for him.

ANG. He gets bullied, yer buy him a DVD player; he goes back to school, yer buy him a PS2; he wants to leave school, yer buy him a bike. Yer've just gotta let him breathe, he's not your project. Yer can't fix everythin'.

PAUL. Not tryin' to fix everythin'.

ANG. You're a good dad.

PAUL. Am I?

ANG. Course yer are. (*Beat.*) Paul –

She stops as BOBBY *comes back inside with more bags.* PAUL *peers out into the yard.*

PAUL. Bob, lock the door, will yer? Not spendin' the best part o' five hundred quid on a load o' new tools fer one o' the bloody clampetts from the campsite to come an' whizz 'em.

BOBBY. Firstly, they're proper tradesmen an' they've got their own tools; and secondly, it's not a campsite, it's council land an' they've got as much right to be there as you have to be here.

PAUL. How d'you know?

Pause.

BOBBY. We did it in school.

PAUL. What lesson's that in?

Pause.

BOBBY. Local community studies.

PAUL. Jesus, no wonder we're overrun with fuckin' half-wits if that's the sort of thing they're teachin' yer. Since when have Gyppos been part of the local community?

ANG. Calm down, will yer, Paul? Sound like a fuckin' spokesman for the *Daily Mail*.

PAUL. 'Local community studies', oh come on, Angela . . . Here y'are . . . Local Community Studies homework for yer Bob, go the offy at the top of our street and get us two cans o' Guinness.

PAUL *pulls a tenner out of his pocket and hands it to* BOBBY.

BOBBY. Can I keep the change?

PAUL. Go 'ead then.

Silence. BOBBY *exits.*

Root of all evil, me arse.

Pause. PAUL *sits down at the table with the paper.*

ANG. Paul.

PAUL. Mmm?

ANG. I'm late.

PAUL. Give me two minutes an' I'll give yer a lift.

ANG. Not for work.

PAUL. Eh?

ANG. I don't mean I'm late for work, Paul. I mean . . . I'm late.

Pause. PAUL *puts the paper down.*

PAUL. How long?

ANG. Two days . . . but anyway. I'm late. (*Beat.*) I'm never late, am I? I'm like clockwork.

PAUL. Have yer bought a test?

ANG. No. Listen . . . I don't wanna. I'm just gonna wait a bit.

PAUL. Are yer sure?

ANG. Few more days. I don't wanna tempt fate. (*Beat.*) I know it's daft.

PAUL. S'not daft.

ANG. I did get these, though.

She reaches into one of the bags and pulls out a tiny box. She opens it. Inside are a tiny pair of booties.

PAUL. Angela.

ANG. I know, I know. (*Beat.*) Look at them, though.

PAUL *takes them and holds them in his hand.*

PAUL. Size o'them.

ANG. They're gorgeous, aren't thee?

He pulls ANG *onto his knee.*

PAUL. Let's just wait, eh? Try not to get too excited.

ANG. I will but . . . I can't help it. (*Beat.*) I feel different. S'like . . . butterflies in me belly. I had that wi' Bobby.

PAUL. Put them away, babe, eh? Put them away an' we'll wait.

ANG. Okay.

ANG puts them back in the box. They hug.

Scene Five

Curzon Park. ELLIE *sits at the table while* MARGARET *cooks; she's juggling pots and pans, getting into a bit of a state and nosing out of the window at the same time.*

MARGARET. I think it's terrible what Patrick and Kathleen are doin wi' the outside o' their trailer. Have yer seen it? Like a royal flower show or somethin'.

ELLIE. If thee like it.

MARGARET. Like a bloody jungle. I called round yesterday, couldn't find the door fer leaves trailin' all over the place. Practically had my eye out wi' a piece o' plastic ivy.

ELLIE. It's their home.

MARGARET. Stupid. Like a nature reserve.

ELLIE. I like it. Bit o' green.

MARGARET. It's all plastic.

ELLIE. It's still green. Where else round here do yer see any green? Warehouses and Esso garages.

MARGARET. Well, I s'pose.

MARGARET inspects the contents of a pan.

Ah bollocks, would yer look at that?

ELLIE. Margaret, let me do something.

MARGARET. It's all under control.

ELLIE. Are yer sure?

MARGARET. Positive. (*She burns her hand on a pan handle.*) Aah fuck yer, yer little bastard. (*Beat.*) Jesus.

ELLIE. Yer need to put a tea towel round that handle. It gets scorchin'.

MARGARET. I noticed. (*Beat.*) What time they come back usually?

ELLIE (*looking at the clock*). About ten minutes ago.

MARGARET. Shite.

ELLIE. Margaret, come an' sit down. I'll take over.

MARGARET. I don't want yer takin' over. I've come t'help. (*Pause.*) Yer da needs t'see what an asset I am.

MARGARET *knocks a glass from the worktop and it shatters onto the floor.*

Aah fer fuck's sake, yer little bastard.

ELLIE *stands and gets a small brush and pan from the cupboard.* MARGARET *takes them off her and ushers her back to her seat. She sweeps up the glass and puts it in the bin.*

One less for washin', anyway.

She brings a pot of stew over to the table and sets it down.

Besides, yer need a break.

ELLIE. I'm all right.

MARGARET. Yer a young woman, yer not a middle-aged wife. Yer've been through a lot, yer should be havin' some fun your age . . . not stuck indoors sweatin' over the cooker.

ELLIE. I do have fun.

Margaret looks interested. She sits down.

MARGARET. Do yer*? (Beat.)* Who with?

ELLIE. Not that sorta fun.

MARGARET. An' what's wrong with tha' sorta fun?

ELLIE. Margaret.

MARGARET. I'm teasin' yer. (*Beat.*) Sort of.

The door opens and FELIX *and* BOBBY *enter.*

Another second an' it would've been in the bin.

FELIX. Bad timin'.

FELIX *walks over and inspects the pan of food.*

MARGARET. It's yer favourite.

FELIX. The way *Winnie* does it, yeah . . .

MARGARET. Aah well, make do and mend, eh? Better than nothin'.

DANIEL *enters sulkily, slamming the door shut behind him. He pushes past* BOBBY *and slumps on the couch.*

ELLIE. Coat.

DANIEL *pulls his coat off and throws it on the floor.* ELLIE *shoots him a look and he snatches it up huffily before hanging it up.*

MARGARET (*to* BOBBY). Son, d'yer like Irish Stew?

BOBBY. Is it like English stew?

MARGARET. Exactly the same. Only this is much better.

BOBBY. Yeah . . . please. Thanks. (*Beat.*) Thank you.

MARGARET. Lovely manners.

FELIX (*shooting a look over at* DANIEL, *who is sitting with his arms crossed, sulking*). Great little worker n'all, aren't yer son? Worked like a trojan today. No stoppin' him.

BOBBY. Nice one, Mr O'Connor.

FELIX. Great little trooper.

BOBBY. It was quite hard at first but . . . I sort of really got into it in the end.

FELIX. Yer a natural.

BOBBY. Daniel worked dead hard too, didn't he?

FELIX *is silent.* DANIEL *stands and pushes past* BOBBY *to go into the bedroom.*

MARGARET. Daniel, this is ready, sit down.

DANIEL. I'm goin' in my room fer a bit.

MARGARET. Yer need t'eat.

DANIEL. I'm not hungry.

FELIX. Sit.

Everyone squeezes in around the table while MARGARET *dishes out the food. They start to eat. There is an uncomfortable silence.*

BOBBY. Y'all right, Dan?

FELIX. He's fine.

Silence.

BOBBY. I saw someone get their head knocked off by a bus once.

MARGARET. Jaysus . . . D'yer mind while we're eatin' like?

BOBBY. Sorry . . . it wasn't . . . well not knocked off, but their face was all smashed in. Thee broke the windscreen. There was blood all over it. His nose was all mashed up. Me mum

35

was screamin' her head off because we were out shoppin'
and me Dad had gone off in a huff, he hates shoppin' like,
and me mum thought it was him. She was like, 'Oh my
God, is it yer dad?' I legged over to see even though I knew
it wasn't him. He had a yellow polo neck on, the man.
(*Pause.*) Me dad had a blue T-shirt on yer see, so I knew it
wasn't.

MARGARET. Yes well. Good then, eh?

Silence.

ELLIE. Was he dead?

BOBBY. Who?

ELLIE. Yer yella polo neck man.

BOBBY. I don't think so.

Pause.

Sometimes when I just think of something I have to say it.

MARGARET. Thee have a name fer that. (*Beat.*) Yer can get
medication for it, y'know?

BOBBY. No, it's not . . . It's just. I just do it sometimes.

DANIEL. Just do it all fuckin' day long, more like.

MARGARET. Language at the table.

Silence.

DANIEL. I've finished . . . Can I go?

MARGARET. Yer've hardly touched it.

DANIEL. I'm not hungry.

BOBBY. It's really nice this, thanks, Margaret.

DANIEL. Aah, will yer put a sock in it, yer little creep.

ELLIE. Daniel, pack it in.

BOBBY. What've I done?

DANIEL. He's doin' me fuckin' head in.

FELIX *clips* DANIEL *over the head, not too hard.*

FELIX. Language at the fuckin' table.

DANIEL. What's he even doin' here, anyway?

BOBBY *sits in stunned silence.*

FELIX. A damn sight more than you have lately, yer lazy little
shite.

36

ELLIE. Da.

MARGARET. Will you stop wi' your pickin' and bickerin',
Felix, fer Jaysus' sake.

DANIEL. Yer wouldn't speak t'me like that if me mam was
here, would yer?

FELIX. I'll speak t'yer how I like, whether she's here or not.

*FELIX's phone starts to ring. ELLIE is nearest and only
she notices. She picks it up and moves to the other end of
the trailer, one finger in her ear, straining to listen.*

DANIEL. Like you care anyway, yer couldn't give a shit . . .
can't even be arsed t'go an' see her.

FELIX. Wha' did yer say?

MARGARET. Felix, leave it, fer Christsake, will yer just –

DANIEL. I said, 'Like you give a shit' . . . are yer deaf?

*FELIX squares up to DANIEL. MARGARET jumps in
between them. BOBBY ducks out of the way and stands by
the door. ELLIE puts the phone down. She is shaking. She
goes over to FELIX and DANIEL and reaches a hand out.*

MARGARET. Don't you dare raise a hand t'him.

ELLIE. Da . . .

DANIEL. Go on, why don't yer jus' gi' me a right good
thump.

ELLIE stands holding the phone out. She is crying.

MARGARET. An' yer can stop antagonising him too,
Daniel . . . yer like a red rag t'a bull.

FELIX. Get out me sight, I can't even stand t' look at yer.

DANIEL. Well let me get past then.

ELLIE (*crying*). Stop –

*They stop and turn to face ELLIE, who is still holding the
phone out. She is sobbing.*

A woman's called. From the hospital.

Interval.

Scene Six

BOBBY *and* DANIEL. *Otterspool.*

BOBBY. There was only three days left so . . . everyone's
running around. (*Beat.*) Actually, they weren't running, it was
all calm. It was just, that's the way it was. (*Pause.*) There
were three days left so . . . yer couldn't really do anything
about it. People were . . . giving stuff away but they didn't
know what for, coz it wasn't any use to anyone now. They're
all in the same boat. But they wanna do it anyway, coz they
need to be doing something. Like they think they're helpin'
but there's no point buying things or selling things. Shops
are open and people are still goin' in but it's all talkin' and
no queues. (*Pause.*) Nobody's arguin' or givin' each other
shit coz . . . what is there to say, yer know? Apart from how
frightened yer are or how much you love someone or who
yer wish yer could see but there's not enough time and . . .
it sort of makes everyone the same. (*Pause.*) Go on.

DANIEL. Eh?

BOBBY. What's yours?

DANIEL. Ah, do I have to?

BOBBY. Yeah. It's a swap.

Pause. DANIEL *thinks.*

DANIEL. I'm in the middle of the sea on one o' them
whatd'yercallits – wha's the name for 'em? A –

BOBBY. A boat.

DANIEL. No. Not a fuckin' boat . . . I wouldn't forget wha'a
boat's called, would I? Do I look like an eejit? (*Beat.*) A lilo.

BOBBY. Doin' what?

DANIEL. Just floating, that's all. (*Beat.*) Underneath a big
black sky. (*Beat.*) Well, not black exactly but not blue
either. Just kind of no colour. If you can think of the colour
of nothing. (*Pause.*) Dirty dish water. So . . . it's sort of dark
but light at the same time. (*Beat.*) I can definitely see the
shape of me hand in the water and I can see beneath the
water. Even though there's nothing there. Yer can tell that
there's nothing there.

BOBBY. And?

DANIEL. That was it.

BOBBY. Nothing happened?

DANIEL. I was lying on a lilo in the middle of the sea. And it's the end o' the world. That's not nothin'. Tha's quite a big fuckin' thing.

BOBBY. Mine lasted for ages. It was like a proper film.

DANIEL. Mine lasted for ages, but I was just floatin' and thinkin'.

BOBBY. But how did you know it was the end of the world?

DANIEL. I just did. You know, don't yer? In a dream, like. Coz it's your own head yer in. (*Beat.*) Yer don't need a runnin' commentary tellin' yer what's come before. Yer know already.

BOBBY. So. The whole world got covered. Like, massive buildings. Skyscrapers. And mountains . . . got covered in water and you only had a lilo, but you were all right?

DANIEL. Yeah.

BOBBY. As if. There's no way that'd happen.

DANIEL. Tha's the fuckin' entire point. (*Beat.*) It's a dream.

BOBBY. Didn't yer wanna just jump off the lilo and drown yerself?

DANIEL. No. I was just floatin'. (*Pause.*) It was quite nice really. (*Beat.*) I think I knew the lilo wouldn't last that long. It was one of those really cheap ones, like you get outside shops in Blackpool. (*Beat.*) By the time I woke up, the water was startin' to get into me eyes.

BOBBY. Did you feel sad?

DANIEL. Not so much, actually. I wasn't that bothered. I just thought it was . . .

BOBBY. What?

DANIEL. I dunno. Jus' . . . interestin' or somethin'. (*Beat.*) In the dream I couldn't swim. But it didn't really bother me like. I jus' let meself . . . it didn't bother me. (*Silence.*) I like sittin' here when it's blowin' a gale. When the sea's blowin up in yer face. (*Beat.*) Makes me wanna jump in when it's like that. Get chucked about by the waves. Let them carry yer fer miles. (*Pause.*) Just probably drown, though. Everyone'd think yer'd killed yerself when yer hadn't.

Silence.

BOBBY. What was it like, eh? The funeral.

Pause.

DANIEL. Not as bad as I thought it was gonna be. It's as if . . .

BOBBY. What?

DANIEL. Like the mos' terrible thing in the world yer can think of, right . . . that could happen t'yer? It's always worse in yer head, I reckon. Coz it hasn't happened yet, so yer just waitin', dreadin' what it's gonna be like. (*Pause.*) When she wa' in the hospital, I had this feelin' like . . . kept thinkin' about her funeral if she died. Hundreds o'people comin' from all over. How it'd be havin' t'bury her and leave her there an' how we'd all be weepin' and wailin' an' it made me feel sick, yeah? (*Pause.*) But when it actually happened it was . . . happenin'. An' I didn't have no time fer the inside o' me head. (*Beat.*) I had things to do, y'know, and even though it was . . . the day itself wasn't as bad as I thought it wa' gonna be.

Pause.

BOBBY. I went t'church for yer.

DANIEL. Thought yer didn't believe in God?

BOBBY. I don't . . . but I wasn't goin' fer me, was I?

DANIEL. You're a strange one.

Pause.

BOBBY. I just wondered.

DANIEL. Wondered what?

BOBBY. If anything was gonna happen. If I felt different or something. Like I belonged. Like thee say yer feel when yer 'find God' an' everythin' fits into place.

DANIEL. Yer never found him though, eh?

BOBBY. No. (*Beat.*) I found a quid under the bench.

DANIEL. Pew.

BOBBY. I put in the box for the spazzys. (*Pause.*) I stayed for the service. It was all right. I never sung or nothin' –

Silence.

Some of them songs aren't that bad, are thee? (*Pause.*) How's everyone else?

DANIEL. Terrible. I can't stick it at home at the moment. It's always rammed wi' people. Can't get no peace. An' me da's in a state. Spent every last penny on the funeral. Him and Margaret at each other's throats and Ellie's cryin' all the time and I jus' feel like I'm . . . I jus' don't wanna be there fer a bit.

BOBBY. It'll get better.

Pause.

DANIEL. Could I stay at yours?

BOBBY. What?

DANIEL. Can I stay at yours . . . even fer like, a night or somethin'?

Silence.

Can I? On the floor like?

BOBBY. I don't think –

DANIEL. Thought yer wanted to be me friend.

BOBBY. I do. It's just . . . it might all blow it up, mightn't it? School an' that. Thee might get suss about it.

DANIEL. No thee won't. We can jus' go straight up t'yer room, can't we? D'yer mates get the third degree when thee come round?

BOBBY. I haven't got any.

DANIEL. Well, there yer go. They'll be made up, won't thee? They'll stop frettin' so much about yer bein' a weirdo.

BOBBY. Thee just worry. (*Beat.*) I dunno.

Pause.

DANIEL. What's the big issue, like?

BOBBY. Nothin'.

DANIEL. Spend enough time hangin' round ours.

BOBBY. I know.

DANIEL. Yer ashamed or somethin'?

BOBBY. What of?

DANIEL. Me.

BOBBY. Don't talk stupid.

Pause.

DANIEL. Fuckin' bollocks to yer.

BOBBY. Don't be like that.

DANIEL. Not bein' like anythin'.

BOBBY. It's rubbish in ours anyway. Yer wouldn't wanna go there.

DANIEL. Thought yer had a PS2?

BOBBY. I could bring it round to yours. Yer can borrow it.

DANIEL. Might not get it back. Know what them Gyppos are like.

BOBBY. Shut up.

DANIEL. So yer ma and da haven't got a problem wi' it then? Us livin' right opposite.

BOBBY. No. Not really. (*Pause.*) It's me dad more than her. (*Beat.*) He's just a whopper. I told yer, didn't I? He doesn't mean any harm, like. He's all talk. Just moans about everything. It's all hot air.

DANIEL. If I stayed fer a night or so he could meet me, couldn't he? Change his mind. Just for a night or two. I can't stick it back there, s'like world war three.

BOBBY. What d'yer think it's like in ours then? I'm surprised they're both still alive. (*Beat.*) I'm not ashamed.

Silence.

Daniel . . .

DANIEL. I heard yer.

Silence.

Might jus' get off, anyway. Leave. Find me own work.

BOBBY. Where to?

DANIEL *shrugs.*

For good?

DANIEL. Dunno. (*Beat.*) Move about a bit. See stuff.

BOBBY. On yer own?

DANIEL. Yeah.

BOBBY. Aah, don't get off.

DANIEL. What's keepin' me round here?

Pause.

BOBBY. Could I come with yer?

DANIEL. Why?

BOBBY. Coz . . .

Pause.

DANIEL. Yer not like . . . queer, are yer?

BOBBY. Gay? No.

DANIEL. Right.

BOBBY. But even if I was . . .

DANIEL. Even if yer was what?

BOBBY. There's nothin' wrong wi' bein' a bender, y'know.

DANIEL *looks at* BOBBY *incredulously.*

There isn't.

DANIEL. It's fuckin' gross.

BOBBY. Aah no, yer've gotta sort that out.

DANIEL. I got nothin' against them personally or anythin' –

BOBBY. I've heard people say tha' about you. It's just a
bullshit way of sayin' thee think they're better than yer.

DANIEL. I don't think I'm better than no one.

BOBBY. Well, don't talk shite then. (*Beat.*) It's too easy.

Silence.

DANIEL. Yer probably wouldn't take to it, anyway.

BOBBY. Being gay?

DANIEL. Travellin'.

BOBBY. Yeah, I would.

DANIEL. How d'yer know?

BOBBY. Coz I would. (*Pause.*) Reckon I could be a Traveller,
me. A proper one like.

DANIEL. Fuck off.

BOBBY. I could.

DANIEL. S'like sayin' yer gonna be fuckin' . . . Chinese all
of a sudden . . . Yer born a Traveller. Stuck wi' it. Same
way yer stuck wi' curly hair or goofy teeth. Yer don't
choose it . . . unless yer become one o' them new age eejits
wi' rainbow coloured jumpers and rats on bits o' string.

BOBBY. I could be a New Age Irish Traveller.

DANIEL. You don't 'alf talk shite sometimes.

BOBBY. Is it coz yer wouldn't want me to?

Pause.

DANIEL. I dunno . . . nah, I just . . . (*Pause.*) I'm not goin' anywhere anyway. Trapped in this shithole same as you.

BOBBY. I'm not trapped.

DANIEL. Why yer still here then?

BOBBY. Just waitin'.

Silence.

Scene Seven

The following morning. FELIX sits on the steps of the trailer, wearing jeans and a jumper. He is smoking and staring into space. MARGARET comes out and sits down beside him. She lights up a cigarette herself.

MARGARET. D'yer mind?

FELIX. Why d'yer care about me mindin' all of a sudden? Yer behind me everywhere I turn anyway.

Silence. MARGARET turns to go inside the trailer, then sits back down.

MARGARET. No joy, then.

FELIX. Joy?

MARGARET. Nothin' doin' on the jobs front like?

FELIX. Yeah, Jesus I got them comin' out me ears. Inundated I am wi' people wantin' stuff doin'. Bitin' me hand off, thee are . . . S'why I'm sat here in me best jumper wi' sixty-five pee in me arse pocket.

MARGARET. Just take it, Felix.

Silence.

Felix –

FELIX. Leave it.

MARGARET. Fuckin' . . . stubborn as the day's long. What's the alternative then, eh? Livin' on fresh air? Yer've spent every last penny on the funeral.

FELIX. I'll get some money.

MARGARET. How?

FELIX. I just will. I'll find it. (*Beat.*) I don't want your money, Margaret.

MARGARET. An' what's wrong wi' my fuckin' money?

FELIX. I'm not a charity case.

MARGARET. It's not charity. It's a loan. (*Beat.*) I expect it back. Every last penny. I'll be countin'.

FELIX. Aye, I bet yer will. An' yer'll love that, won't yer? Get yer claws in that bit more. Remindin' me all the time what yer've done fer me like the great fuckin' martyr that yer are. It won't buy yer the right to plant yer feet under the table, yer know.

MARGARET. You've got a fuckin' cruel tongue on yer, Felix O'Connor.

FELIX. I'm just gettin' warmed up.

MARGARET. So am I. An' I tell yer, I can give as good an' fuckin' more, sunshine. I've been bitin' my tongue fer a fair while, so one more fuckin' jab from you an' I'll be only too happy to let rip.

FELIX. Will yer now? I'd like t'see yer try.

DANIEL *enters.* FELIX *goes inside the trailer.*

MARGARET. All right, love?

DANIEL *tries to get past her into the trailer but she winds him up by playfully sliding left and right to get in his way.*

DANIEL. Margaret, will yer pack it in?

MARGARET. Lord above, it talks! An' there wa' me thinkin' yer'd turned into one of them mutes.

DANIEL. Can I get past?

MARGARET. Why don't yer sit down wi' me fer a while?

DANIEL. Wha' for?

MARGARET. A chat. (*Beat.*) A catch-up. I could put the kettle on.

DANIEL. Wha's happened?

MARGARET. Jesus . . . does there have t'be a crisis to have a sit down wi' me nephew?

DANIEL *sits on the step beneath* MARGARET.

(*Holding out the cigarette packet.*) D'yer smoke?

DANIEL. What are yer on about? Yer know I don't.

MARGARET. Aye well, I thought yer might a bin lyin', yer know. Yer a bit old fer sneakin' off fera sly one now though, aren't yer?

45

DANIEL. I don't smoke. Don't like it.

MARGARET *stubs the cigarette out.*

MARGARET. What yer bin doin' wi' yerself today then?

DANIEL. Nothin'.

MARGARET. An' how was that?

DANIEL. All right.

Silence.

MARGARET. How yer feelin', son?

DANIEL. All right.

MARGARET. Good. (*Beat.*) Good.

Silence.

Work's not goin' so well though, eh?

DANIEL. No.

MARGARET. Pick up soon though, yeah?

DANIEL. Yeah.

Silence.

MARGARET. Well this is nice, isn't it? Good old chin wag. Can't beat 'em.

DANIEL. Margaret, I'm tired, s'all.

MARGARET. Look son, I'm just . . . I'm goin' t'have to go back soon. There's not much reason fer me t'stay round here no more and I think yer da's gettin' right t' the end of his fuckin' tether, an' I . . . jus' want yer t'know . . .

DANIEL. Know what?

MARGARET. That I love yer like. You an' Ellie both. I fuckin' love the pair o'yer t'death.

Silence.

Yer da thinks I wanna take over. Take the place o' your – it isn't like that. (*Pause.*) I jus' want yer t'know . . . I'm there like. I'm always there. Don't lose touch, will yer? Don't let him persuade yer that I'm some old dragon. Don't leave it months an' months, will yer? (*Beat.*) If yer need me . . .

DANIEL. Yeah.

MARGARET. If yer wanna talk like. About yer mam. About anythin'.

Silence.

Then yer can like.

Silence. There is a possibility that DANIEL *is about to say something but before he does so* BOBBY *walks into view. He is wearing his school uniform, holding a football.* MARGARET *notices him first.*

Jesus, here's yer shadow.

BOBBY. Should I . . . is it a bad time? (*Pause.*) D'yer want me t'go?

MARGARET. It's always a bad time round here at the moment, sunshine, but I wouldn't worry about it. (*She stands.*) Here y'are, I've kept it warm fer yer.

MARGARET *exits.*

BOBBY. Look at this.

He starts to do keep-ups and manages a few more than usual before the ball rolls off. DANIEL *looks distinctly unimpressed.*

Gettin' better, aren't I?

DANIEL. Expert.

BOBBY. Brought yer somethin'.

BOBBY *rummages in his bag and brings out his PS2. He hands it to* DANIEL *but he doesn't take it.*

Yer can borrow it fer a bit.

DANIEL *takes the PS2.*

DANIEL. Ta.

BOBBY. S'all right. (*Pause.*) I thought of somethin'.

DANIEL. To do with what?

BOBBY. Work. (*Beat.*) I know how t'get some for yer. For us.

DANIEL. What sorta stuff?

BOBBY. Oddjobs . . . bit o' paintin', that sorta thing.

DANIEL. When?

BOBBY. Whenever suits you and yer dad.

DANIEL. Well, we're hardly busy doin' much else, are we? Apart from him drinkin' but he's run outa cash fer that n'all. (*Beat.*) Fill us in then.

BOBBY (*playing with the football*). Come an' have a game then, I'll tell yer on the field.

DANIEL. Can't yer just tell us here? I can't be arsed wi' footy today.

BOBBY. Frightened that I'm gonna whoop yer arse more like.

DANIEL jumps up and tackles the ball from BOBBY. He runs offstage kicking it, with BOBBY chasing after him

Scene Eight

FELIX *and* BOBBY *are painting a wall.*

FELIX. Even strokes now, yer not pebble dashing the fuckin' ting.

BOBBY *continues painting.*

Jesus. (*Pause.*) See what I'm doin'? Up and down. There'll be no fuckin' hairs left on the brush.

They continue.

And yer not covering up fer him?

BOBBY. No. Honestly . . . I dunno where he is.

FELIX. Coz if yer are . . .

BOBBY. I'm not.

FELIX *looks at* BOBBY.

He mighta meant another mate's.

FELIX. Stayin' overnight at another mate's called Bobby. There's a coincidence an' a half for yer, isn't it now?

FELIX *grabs the brush from* BOBBY.

Are yer gonna do it properly or do I have to do it meself?

FELIX *demonstrates, then hands the brush back to* BOBBY.

BOBBY. I could go an' look fer him.

FELIX. Right yeah. Great idea. Leave soft shite here t'do all the graft.

BOBBY. Jus' thought . . . if yer worryin'–

FELIX. Who mentioned worryin'? (*Beat.*) Ragin' more like, but not worryin' . . . he's a grown fella. Can look after himself well enough. Sure that's what he's up to now . . . havin' a good laugh on my time.

Silence. They carry on with the job.

BOBBY. Mr O'Connor?

Silence.

Mr O'Connor?

FELIX. What?

Pause.

BOBBY. I think he's probably . . . I think he just probably
feels . . . (*Pause.*) Like he's . . .

FELIX. Jesus . . . is there somethin' up wi' you? Spit it out.
(*Pause.*) An' can yer not paint an' talk at the same time?

BOBBY. Upset. (*Pause.*) I think he's upset.

FELIX. Oh, do yer now?

BOBBY. Yeah.

FELIX. Right. Why d'yer think that is then?

BOBBY. Why?

FELIX. Yeah. Why?

BOBBY. Because. His mum died.

Pause.

FELIX. No. When was this?

BOBBY. When did she . . . what d'yer –

FELIX. When'd this happen then? His mammy dyin'?

Pause.

BOBBY. Are yer . . . the other week.

FELIX. Did she now? Jesus . . . it must a gone right over my
stupid head. (*Beat.*) What with her only bein' my wife n'all.

BOBBY. I know. I wasn't tryin' to . . . I'm really sorry about it
and I . . . I wasn't tryin' a' . . .

FELIX. Just try to keep yer nose out of stuff where it doesn't
belong, son, all right? Just try not to start tellin' me about
my family. (*Beat.*) I might not be the sharpest tool in the
box like, but I've got a fair idea of what people are feelin'
round here at the moment an' it's somethin' that you don't
know nothin' about. So if yer wanna carry on wi' this, then
grand, but if yer don't, stick that in there – (*Gestures to
paintbrush and bucket.*) and get back t'where you come
from.

Silence. BOBBY *puts the paintbrush back in the bucket
then goes to leave. He takes a few steps then falters and
turns back round. He picks the paintbrush out of the bucket
dips it in the tin of paint and gets back to painting the wall,
this time with a little more vigour than before.*

He'll come back when he's ready. Probably taken hi'self over to the site at Preston or somethin' . . . (*Referring to* BOBBY'*s work.*) Tha's good that. Tha's good . . . Jus' keep . . . keep doin' tha' . . . (*Long pause.*) Think yer'll be all right on yer own fer an hour or two?

BOBBY. Yeah. (*Beat.*) Sound.

FELIX. Yer doin' a good job there.

BOBBY. Ta.

FELIX. Jus' carry on like tha' . . . I won't be too long.

BOBBY. Are yer gonna go and look fer him?

FELIX. Will yer fuckin' shut up an' stop goin' on about Daniel, fer Christ's sake?

Pause.

I got a meetin' wi' someone . . . 'bout a job. (*Beat.*) Keep tha' up. No slackin' coz I'm not around, yeah?

BOBBY. No.

FELIX *leaves. As his footsteps trail off down the entry,* BOBBY *sits, shaking his painting arm. A couple of seconds later the door rattles and opens;* BOBBY *jumps up and grabs the brush. It is* ELLIE.

ELLIE. Sorry.

BOBBY. Thought it was yer Dad.

ELLIE. No, he's well away. (*Beat.*) I've been sat round the corner waitin' fer him t'leave.

BOBBY. How d'yer know he's goin' anywhere?

ELLIE. One o'clock, isn'it?

BOBBY . . . .

ELLIE. Pub time.

BOBBY. Oh right . . . no, he's got a meetin' with someone he said.

ELLIE. Oh aye, he has. (*Beat.*) Meetin' wi' the fuckin' barman. (*Pause.*) Yer not get lunch on this job or somethin'?

BOBBY. He wants this wall done by the time he gets back.

ELLIE. You want yer head testin', you do. Jesus, your da must be some fuckin' nightmare if this is what yer escapin' to. (*Beat.*) Sit back down, yer'll be on yer own fer a while yet.

BOBBY *sits.* ELLIE *drags a crate over and sits beside him.*
She reaches into her bag and pulls out some sandwiches.

Daniel's. They'll only get chucked in the bin if you don't
have them.

BOBBY. He's not turned up then?

ELLIE. Nah.

Silence.

BOBBY. He was talkin' to me the other day . . . we were just
talking about things. About yer mum and . . . stuff.

ELLIE. And?

BOBBY. And he was sayin' that he was gonna get off. Like
leave. Go off on his own or somethin'.

Silence.

I didn't really think he meant it, yer know. An' I'm not even
sayin' that's what he's done. It's only one night, isn't it? Yer
dad was just sayin' then he's probably gone to Preston or
somethin'. I don't reckon he's left, not properly, I think –

ELLIE. I hope he has.

BOBBY. I bet he has, y'know. He's always goin' on about yer
cousins an' everyone there and –

ELLIE. I don't mean Preston.

Pause.

I mean, I hope he's left for good. (*Beat.*) I hope he's stuck
two fingers up to this shitehole and he's legging it as far
away as he can get. Only wish I had the nerve t'do the
same. Good on him.

Silence.

Did he mention anywhere in particular?

BOBBY. No.

Silence. ELLIE *puts her head on her knees.*

Are yer all right?

ELLIE. Yeah.

BOBBY. I think yer dad's really pissed off wi' him.

ELLIE. Me da's really pissed off wi' everyone an' everythin'.
That's what thirty years livin' here does for yer. I don't
wanna be like that but it's hard.

BOBBY. Mmm.

ELLIE. No, don't do that 'mmm' coz yer don't even know.

BOBBY. I was just makin' . . . a listenin' noise.

Pause.

ELLIE. S'just . . . yer have to work that bit harder when people are waiting for yer to fuck it up, d'yer know what I'm sayin'? All people do shit stuff, don't thee? I mean not all people as in everyone, although everyone's not angels . . . but all types of people. D'y'know? Makes no sense. It's all labels. Simple as anything. It wrecks me head. Makes me feel like biting metal. (*Pause.*) Get used to feeling like you owe the world a fuckin' explanation for breathin'. (*Pause.*) Sorry for snappin'.

BOBBY. S'okay.

Pause.

ELLIE. When I saw me mammy. Afterwards like. When she come back home. (*Beat.*) I stood by the door fer a while, just gettin' hold o' meself, kept sayin' over an' over in me head, ''S not really her, yer know wha' she looks like, tha's not her.' Got meself all knotted up expectin' somethin' . . . expectin' her t'look like . . . well y'know, what yer might imagine. Shut me eyes and took a breath an' went to her, opened 'em an' . . . She looked fuckin' gorgeous. (*Pause.*) Like the weight o' the world were off her shoulders. Twenty years younger. Didn't have a wrinkle on her face. (*Pause.*) Always frownin', she wa', me mam. Always had her forehead bunched up like she wa' worried sick about somethin'. (*Beat.*) She jus' looked like everythin' wa' grand. Like it'd all stopped. All the shite. An' I jus' thought . . . is this wha' it takes, like? This is the only peace yer get. She's struggled like a Trojan her whole life an' the best she's ever looked is lyin' in her coffin. (*Beat.*) Some shitty turn-up that is.

Silence.

BOBBY. At least . . .

ELLIE. At least what?

BOBBY. I dunno. (*Beat.*) Sorry.

Pause.

ELLIE. So what's this all about then, really?

BOBBY. How d'yer mean?

ELLIE. This. Bein' here . . . not bein' over there.

BOBBY. I like it.

ELLIE. Yer like workin' yer knackers off for tuppence an'
bein' barked at all day by me arl fella?

BOBBY. I like not havin' to do what's expected of me. Havin'
me mum and dad's idea of what's good for me shoved down
me neck every day.

ELLIE. Thee don't suspect nothin' like?

BOBBY. No reason to, have thee? As long as I tell them they
believe me. Thee just believe whatever's fed to them. About
anythin'. (*Pause.*) I told them that I got a certificate fer
somethin' the other day. That'll shut them up fer a bit.

ELLIE. What if yer mam wants to see it? (*Beat.*) That's the
sort of thing thee want for their boxes.

BOBBY. What boxes?

ELLIE. Their boxes. For when yer grow up and yer don't
come round t'visit no more. She'll sit in her room and look
through yer old exercise books and hold yer baby teeth in
her hands and get the band from around yer wrist from
when yer were born and try an' fit it round hers to feel
closer to yer.

BOBBY. She hasn't got one.

ELLIE. Ah, they all have. It's a universal thing. A box or a
drawer. Or . . . an old handbag that's out of fashion but
proper leather so they keep it in case it comes back in.
(*Beat.*) Somethin' all with little bits of yer in.

BOBBY. She's got one of those conditions.

ELLIE. An illness?

BOBBY. A cleanin' thing. Yer can't put anything down for
longer than five seconds without her chucking it out.

ELLIE. I bet she has somethin'. (*Beat.*) Little lock o' hair or
somethin'.

BOBBY. I don't reckon. She's not like other mums, d'yer
know what I mean?

ELLIE. No one's mam is.

BOBBY. Not in a 'she's so special' way . . . I mean she is
special . . . sometimes. She's just not a mumsy mum.
(*Beat.*) I love her, like.

ELLIE. Big o' yer.

BOBBY. Yer know what I mean.

ELLIE. Yeah well, yer shouldn't take her fer granted.

BOBBY. No.

Pause. ELLIE *surveys the wall.*

ELLIE. Yer've got a bit of a way t'go there, haven't yer?

BOBBY. Yeah, I better get going again.

ELLIE. D'yer want a hand?

BOBBY. Nah, don't be soft.

ELLIE. What, not a girl's job or somethin'?

BOBBY. I'm tryin' a' be polite, that's all.

ELLIE *picks up the brush* FELIX *has been using and dips it into the pot of paint.*

ELLIE. Right, shall I go this way and we work toward each other?

BOBBY. Erm . . . Yeah.

BOBBY *is still sat on the crate.* ELLIE *hands him the other brush.*

ELLIE. Well, come on, then. Not gonna paint itself is it?

BOBBY *stands up. They start to paint.*

Scene Nine

PAUL *and* ANG's *kitchen.* ANG *is frantically cleaning. There is a bin bag on the floor by the table.* PAUL *enters in his work outfit, hangs up his coat. Gets a bottle of lager from the fridge, takes a swig. He looks at the notepad by the telephone.*

PAUL. Angela, what's this?

ANG. If I had eyes stickin' out the back o' me head, Paul, I'd tell yer.

PAUL *puts the pad down in front of* ANG.

It is what it is.

PAUL. Don't be going all Zen on me, 'It is what it is'. Why'd they cancel?

ANG. He didn't really say. Just said thee didn't need it doing no more.

PAUL. That's the third fuckin' one this week, Angela.

ANG. And that's my fault, is it?

PAUL. No . . . why does everything have to turn into us havin' an argument? I'm not saying it's your fault, I'm sayin' why are a load o'jobs gettin' cancelled at the last minute?

ANG. Then reel yer neck in while yer sayin' it. Stop bein' so confrontational.

PAUL. Says fuckin' Boadicea. What else did he say?

ANG. Who?

PAUL (*holding the pad*). The bloke from Sykes Street.

ANG. Nothin' . . . Paul, he doesn't want it doin' no more. End of.

PAUL *picks up an A4 notebook from the countertop. He flicks through the pages.*

PAUL. So . . . his guttering's fucked an' he's beggin' me to fit him in as soon as possible. An' all of a sudden he's decided he doesn't want it doin'.

ANG. Apparently so.

PAUL. I'm not havin' that.

ANG. People are skint. Thee get ideas about gettin' the garden flagged or a new coat o'paint on the house an' thee ring yer up. Then the phone bill comes in an' it's either pay that or get the work done an' get cut off. It's Everton, Paul, not Formby. (*Beat.*) He'll probably call yer back next month when things are better. It's nothin' to do wi' you.

PAUL. I know it's nothin' to do with me. I never thought it was to do wi' me . . . why would it be? I've never had one complaint –

ANG. And breathe.

PAUL. Have I, though?

ANG. No yer haven't, Paul. (*She digs in her handbag and pulls out a small bottle with a dropper on the end.*) Here y'are, have a blast on that.

PAUL. What is it?

ANG. Rescue Remedy. Chills yer out.

PAUL. Did your Pamela nick it from the hozzy for yer?

ANG. No. It's made out of flowers, dickhead. I got it from Holland and Barrett.

PAUL (*reading the bottle*). Clematis and Cherry Plum. Fuckin' hell, Angela, thee see you comin' a mile off, don't thee?

ANG. Two drops on yer tongue. An' I got it fer Bobby, actually. For his exams. Thought it might help.

PAUL. He's in remedial maths. I don't think chewin' a dandelion before he goes into the test's gonna be much help.

ANG. It's for his nerves. And he's not in remedial maths, he's in group C. Yer don't say 'remedial' any more, Paul. No wonder he's got no fuckin' confidence.

PAUL. Thought it might be my fault. (*Beat.*) D'yer ever think, yeah? That he's got no confidence coz you keep tellin' him he's got no confidence? Yer treat him like he's soft.

ANG. I treat him with sensitivity, Paul. Look it up in the dictionary. It's somewhere between sarcastic and sour-faced. (*Beat.*) An' he's sound these days, isn't he? Look at the change in him.

PAUL. Yeah. He's gettin' better.

ANG. He's not ill, Paul.

PAUL. Jesus . . . can I get through two sentences without doin' something wrong? Fuckin' hell, I'm agreeing with yer.

ANG. Whoa, there it goes again . . . fuckin' human giraffe.

PAUL *swigs down the last of the lager and throws the bottle into the bin bag.*

Not in there. (*She jumps up and retrieves the bottle then pulls out a brand new babygro. She shakes the drops of lager off and sniffs it.*) Stinks now.

Pause.

PAUL. What's goin' on, babe?

ANG. Nothin'.

PAUL *starts to pull out items of baby clothing from the bag. He puts them on the table. As he does,* ANG *starts putting them straight back into the bag*

Don't. Just . . . leave it.

PAUL. Where did all this come from?

ANG. Just . . . bits an' bobs I've been pickin' up. Takin' it all to Oxfam in the mornin'. Yer can drop us on yer way to work, can't yer? (*Pause.*) Eh?

PAUL. Yeah.

Silence. PAUL *picks the booties from earlier out of the bag. He stares at* ANG.

ANG. What? (*Beat.*) Stop lookin' at me like that. I'm fine. (*Beat.*) Honestly. I feel fine.

PAUL *goes to hug her. She backs away.*

Don't. Can yer just . . . stick them back in there and tie it up. I don't want Bob lookin' in it.

PAUL *puts the booties back in the bag. Ties the top and puts it by the door.*

PAUL. Where is he, anyway?

ANG. I dunno.

PAUL. It's half ten.

ANG. He's nearly sixteen fer Christ's sake. An' you talk about me wrappin' him in cotton wool?

PAUL. I'm not sayin' he shouldn't be out. I'm just . . . who's he with?

ANG. Mates from school.

PAUL. He hasn't mentioned anyone. (*Beat.*) I haven't heard names.

ANG. It might be a girl.

PAUL. Oh aye, yeah.

ANG. Don't be like that.

PAUL. Bit of a turn-around though, isn't it? Few weeks yer couldn't get him out of his room, now he's never here.

ANG. Well, exactly . . . I think we should count our blessin's, don't you? Means he's out there . . . doin' somethin' he likes.

PAUL. Yeah, drugs.

ANG. Give over.

PAUL. I'm jokin'.

ANG. He's been workin' hard recently . . . gettin' really stuck in at school. Makin' an effort . . . an' it's paid off, hasn't it? He'll be in there now. Gettin' in with people (*Beat.*) It's the beginning for him now. New start.

ANG *opens a cupboard and starts emptying the contents, pots and pans, onto the floor.*

PAUL. What are yer doin' now?

ANG. Jus givin' the cupboards a wipe. (*Beat.*) Thee haven't been done for years.

PAUL. Do it tomorrow.

ANG. I feel like it.

PAUL. I'm gonna go to bed.

> PAUL *stands and waits.* ANG *carries on piling things onto the floor.*

Are yer comin' soon?

ANG. Yeah. (*Beat.*) In a bit.

PAUL. Yer need to take it easy.

> ANG *stops.*

ANG. Why, Paul?

> *Pause.*

PAUL. Night.

> PAUL *leaves, shutting the door behind him. After a couple of moments* ANG *goes over to the binbag and unties it. She take the booties out.*

Scene Ten

Otterspool. Night time. DANIEL *sits alone. After a couple of seconds* BOBBY *enters on his bike. He gets off and sits down. They are silent for a few moments.*

BOBBY. Thought yer'd gone. (*Beat.*) Left like yer said.

> *Silence.*

DANIEL. What you doin' here?

BOBBY. Lookin' fer you.

> DANIEL *shrugs.*

Never finished that job today. (*He laughs.*) Yer arl fella went the pub an' never came back.

> BOBBY *laughs.*

DANIEL. Hilarious.

BOBBY. Ellie gave me a hand. I think she's worried about yer.

DANIEL. Well I'm all right, aren't I?

BOBBY. How come yer didn't go?

DANIEL. I couldn't leave you.

BOBBY. Shurrup.

DANIEL. No money and no van. Makes it a bit awkward. Walked t' the Liver Buildings and got a bus here. Went the Albert Dock, too. (*Beat.*) Yer right, it is shite.

BOBBY. Told yer. (*Silence.*) Let's get off.

BOBBY *stands and picks his bike up.*

DANIEL. I'm all right. Just wanna stay here a bit longer.

BOBBY. It's cold.

DANIEL. I'm okay. Just wanna sit here.

BOBBY *sits back down.*

On me own.

BOBBY. Tough shit.

DANIEL *looks at* BOBBY.

DANIEL. Is it now? If I wanna be on me own, I'll be on me fuckin' own. Go away.

BOBBY. Why yer always doin' that, eh? Makin' out like I annoy yer an' yer can't be arsed wi' me? When, yer know, we have a buzz an' . . . I know yer into hangin' round wi' me. Why are yer a such a moody twat?

DANIEL. Maybe coz me mother just died.

BOBBY. Sorry. I know. I'm sorry, I didn't mean . . . but Daniel, you were like that before she died. When we met and I tried and tried an' sometimes it's boss and I feel like we're really good . . . really good mates. And other times I just wonder why I fuckin' bother.

DANIEL. Coz yer haven't got no one else to hang around wi'.

BOBBY. No I haven't, but d'yer know what? I'd rather have no mates than feel a tit all the time in front of you. (*Beat.*) I'm so sorry about yer mum an' everything that's happenin' . . . I'll leave yer though, if that's what yer want. Just makin' sure you're all right.

BOBBY *picks up his bike again and goes to get on it.*

DANIEL. Hang on.

BOBBY *stops.*

Don't mind yer sittin' here. (*Beat.*) If yer don't fuckin' rabbit on, like . . . just enjoyin' the peace.

BOBBY *gets off his bike and sits down again.*

BOBBY. As apologies go it's not the greatest, like – but I'll let
yer off.

They sit in silence.

DANIEL. Had one o' yer stupid dreams last night. (*Pause.*)
Some big earthquake or somethin' . . . an explosion.
Could've bin terrorists, I'm not sure. Anyway, it wasn't
water. Took us all by surprise so there wasn't no time for
nothin'. It was just . . . normal, then a shock an' a big black
cloud . . . like people say on the news. And I'm out
somewhere, walkin' on me own . . . maybe it's meant t'be
here, like, I'm not sure, but when that happens I start
runnin' an' I can't see me hand in front o' me face or
nothin', but then I get t' roads an' it's clearin' a bit an' I can
see that everythin's just fuckin' . . . destroyed. Gone.
There's bodies and roofs missing and beds in the street and
kids' toys up trees or what's left o' trees an' I get t'the site
an' me heart's in me fuckin' mouth like I'm so scared o'
what I'm gonna find but I turn into the gates and it's all just
normal. The kids are all playin' out, an' there's some big
fuckin' argument goin' on between two o' the trailers about
nothin' much . . . usual shite. Someone's said somethin'
thee shouldn't an' someone else is threatenin' t'spark them.
An' the big black cloud's just . . . gone. Disappeared.
(*Pause.*) I get t'our trailer an' I open the door an' me
mammy's stood there, peelin' spuds. I'm trippin' over
meself tryin' a tell her what's just happened wi' the
explosion or whatever an' the bodies and the toys in trees
an' she goes, 'Daniel, sit down, yer big daft eejit, it was just
a dream, son.'

Silence. BOBBY *puts an arm around* DANIEL, *who moves
swiftly away.* BOBBY *empties his pockets and counts
money out.*

BOBBY. Have yer eaten anythin' today.

DANIEL *shakes his head.*

Wanna go the chippy?

Silence.

I'll buy it if you give us a seater.

DANIEL *stands and takes the bike off* BOBBY. *He climbs
on and* BOBBY *stands on the back. They ride off.*

Scene Eleven

The next morning. FELIX *is up a ladder, fiddling about with some guttering, swearing and muttering under his breath. He doesn't notice* PAUL *enter.* PAUL *knocks on the back door, then notices* FELIX. PAUL *watches him for a moment or two before speaking.*

FELIX. Aah Jaysus . . . by the curse o' God –

PAUL. Yer all right there, mate?

> FELIX *looks down.*

FELIX. Wassat?

PAUL. I said. (*Beat.*) Are you all right up there, mate?

FELIX. Yes. Fine. Grand, thanks. (*Beat.*) Can I help yer?

PAUL. Just looked like you were strugglin' a bit.

FELIX. No, it wa' just . . . it's fine. I'm all right. (*Beat.*) Cheers.

PAUL. Right. Sound.

FELIX. He's at work.

PAUL. Sorry?

FELIX. He's gone t'work.

PAUL. Who?

FELIX. Mr . . . whatsit. Fella lives here. That's who yer after, right?

PAUL. Er yeah. I did want a word wi'him, like.

FELIX. Aah well. He's not here. Neither's she. Mrs Whatsit.

PAUL. Right. Okay. Ta.

> PAUL *stays. He stares up at* FELIX *for a few moments before speaking.*

> Doin' a little job there then, mate? Gutterin'?

FELIX. It'd look that way. (*Silence.*) Anythin' else yer were wantin'?

PAUL. Nah, just thought yer were in a bit o' trouble, like. Heard yer when I came in. I know what that's like when yer working on yer own, up a fuckin' ladder and yer've got yer hands full, an' yer just need help fer a second. It's a bastard.

FELIX. Good o' yer but I'm okay, thanks.

PAUL. Just thought I'd ask, like.

FELIX. Right. Cheers.

> FELIX *carries on.* PAUL *stays watching.*

PAUL. Tricky fuckers, aren't thee?

FELIX. Wassat?

PAUL (*shouting*). Tricky fuckers. Gutters.

FELIX. Aye.

PAUL. How long yer bin doin' this for, then?

FELIX. Coupla hours.

PAUL. Nah, I mean, yer know . . . this line o' work, how long yer been in the business?

FELIX. Years. Years an' years. (*Beat.*) I hope yer don't mind, like, but I've got another job on this afternoon and I've gotta get this done be then. Yer sort o' puttin' me off me stride, like.

PAUL. Bit ambitious that, mate. I'd say there was a coupla days left in that job. Don't wanna go rushin' it like, do yer? Get a reputation as a cowboy.

FELIX. I'm nearly there. Look, I'm not bein' fuckin' funny –

PAUL. Good to be busy, though, isn't it? (*Beat.*) Where's the other job?

FELIX. Wha' the fuck's it got to do wi' you?

PAUL. Here y'are mate, don't be like that when I'm bein' civil to yer. I'm just askin' yer a simple question. Makin' conversation.

> *Pause.*

FELIX. Copple Street.

PAUL. Copple Street?

FELIX. Aye.

PAUL. No way. I was booked to do a job in Copple Street. Painting the outside of the house. Thee cancelled on me last minute. Fuckin' mad, that.

FELIX. What's so mad about it?

PAUL. Bit of coincidence, isn't it? Maybe coincidence isn't the right word.

> FELIX *has stopped work now and is making his way down the ladder. He reaches the bottom and stands opposite PAUL.*

FELIX. Why?

PAUL. I think yer know why, mate.

FELIX. I don't do riddles, I'm afraid, mister, you're gonna have to just come wi' it in plain English.

PAUL. That's a fuckin' laugh comin' from you, isn't it?

FELIX. Yer wastin' my time.

PAUL. No this is *my* fuckin' time you're wastin'. An' my money. Taking people for a fuckin' ride.

FELIX. I'm doin' a good job.

PAUL. Yer doin' *my* job.

FELIX. Fuck off.

PAUL. Sorry?

FELIX. Yer heard me. Go an' get yer own fuckin' job an' let me make a livin' in peace.

PAUL. Fuckin' Paddy's an' Poles, all the fuckin' same. There's a certain code of conduct that *English* tradesmen have, Mick. Undercutting isn't on it.

FELIX. Me name's Felix O'Connor.

PAUL. I don't care if yer name's fuckin' Mike Tyson . . . Your lot are fuckin' stealin' work away from under me nose. An' I tell yer, mate, this is the last time it happens.

FELIX. I haven't fuckin' stolen nothin' off yer.

PAUL. I live over the road from yer. I see everythin' that goes on –

FELIX. I got this job meself.

PAUL. An' yer spoke to Mr Whatsit, did yer?

FELIX. Me son did. He arranged it. We work together. It's a family business.

PAUL. Business? (*Pause.*) And this is how yer run yer business is it, yeah? Do it in half the time. For what . . . half the price? Yer'd be a mug to refuse that, wouldn't yer? Fuckin' bigger mug t' get the likes o' you onto it, though.

FELIX. I think there's been a misunderstandin'.

PAUL. I can't see that, can you?

FELIX. I got hired t'do a job an' that's exactly wha' I'm doin'.

PAUL. Fuckin' pikey scum.

FELIX. Watch your step there, sunshine.

PAUL. Sunshine?

FELIX. I know fuck all about undercuttin' yer. But I tell yer something . . . meetin' yer I don't feel too bad about it.

PAUL. I'm fuckin' warnin' yer –

FELIX. I didn't set this fuckin' job up.

PAUL. Hold on . . . five minutes ago yer did. So yer wanna just keep a check on the bullshit yer comin' out with –

DANIEL *bursts into the yard carrying a plastic bag from the chippy.*

DANIEL. Thee never had mushy peas so I got yer curry instead. (*He stops and looks up at his father and* PAUL.) Wha'?

FELIX. Who d'yer speak to about this job, Daniel?

DANIEL. What d'yer mean?

PAUL. He means –

FELIX. Keep fuckin' out.

PAUL. Here y'are, mate, I'm not fuckin' standin' fer –

FELIX. How'd yer get this job, Daniel?

DANIEL *stands for a moment, dumbstruck. Suddenly* PAUL *moves towards him.* DANIEL *throws the bag of chippy food at* PAUL *and legs it out onto the entry, with* PAUL *following closely behind. After a moment's pause* FELIX *follows.*

Scene Twelve

MARGARET *and* ELLIE *are sitting in the trailer.*

MARGARET (*looking out of the window*). Look at that . . . it's an absolute disgrace. Unbelievable.

ELLIE (*craning her neck*). What is?

MARGARET *marches straight out of the trailer.*

MARGARET (*shouting, offstage*). Bugger off . . . go on, sod off, yer cheeky shower o' bastards before I ring the police. Get out of it. Dump yer shite in yer own shitty back yard. (*She comes back into the trailer, shuts the door calmly and goes back into the kitchen.*) That's it. That's done it. (*Beat.*)

Bye bye. Well done, Margaret. Cheeky bastards. Think they can blame it all on us an' get away wi' it. I tell yer somethin', not while I'm around. Youse lot might be happy to just let things roll over yer but I tell yer somethin' –

ELLIE. I'm not lettin' anythin' roll over me. I can't get a word in edgeways, s'all.

Beat.

MARGARET. I get angry about things. It's good t'get angry about things, y'know? Nothin' gets done without a little bit o' passion.

Pause.

ELLIE. I wish yer weren't goin', Margaret.

MARGARET. Aah come on, yer'll be glad t'see the back o' me. Witterin' on, stickin' me nose in yer business all the time.

ELLIE. No, I won't. I'll miss yer. (*Pause.*) Margaret, can yer not stay, like?

MARGARET. Ellie love, I've fought me corner hard enough t'stay this long. There's no reason any more. I wanted to be here for yer an' now . . . tings have t'get back t'normal.

ELLIE. Are yer missin' Kent?

Pause.

MARGARET. Yeah. Yes, I am.

ELLIE. I was thinkin', right . . . I could come down, couldn't I? Even like next week or somethin', I could come down an' visit yer, stay fer a week or somethin' . . . it's ages since I've been an' the weather's getting nice an' everythin'. I could, couldn't I?

MARGARET. I'd love yer to . . . course, it's just –

ELLIE. Just wha'?

There is a little knock on the door and BOBBY *enters. He sits down, puffed and out of breath.*

BOBBY. Hiya.

ELLIE. You bin sacked or somethin'?

BOBBY. It's only a little job. Thee don't need me today.

ELLIE. That's a cheek, innit? You set 'em up, then yer out on your ear.

BOBBY. Only fer today. D'yer mind if I stay here till thee finish?

65

MARGARET. Jesus, when d'yer break up from school,
Bobby?

BOBBY. Not long.

ELLIE. What are yer huffin' an' puffin' about?

BOBBY. Got me first exam this afternoon. Me Mum kept
goin' on about wantin' to drive me in, couldn't shut her up.
Got her to drop me off round the corner and walked all the
way back.(*Beat.*) Knackered.

The door swings open violently and DANIEL *enters. He is
holding one hand over his head and rushes past everyone to
the bedroom. He locks the door.* ELLIE *stands outside.*

ELLIE. Daniel, what's goin' on? What's the matter?

DANIEL. Nothin'.

ELLIE. Open the door.

DANIEL. I'm all right, just leave me a second.

ELLIE. Open the door, Daniel.

MARGARET, *oblivious to what's happening, is laughing
loudly at the television.*

MARGARET (*to TV*). That told yer, yer daft bastard.

ELLIE. Daniel.

MARGARET *switches the TV off.*

MARGARET. Wha's goin' on now?

ELLIE. Daniel, open this door.

BOBBY *joins* ELLIE *at the door.*

BOBBY. Dan . . . yer all right?

The door opens and DANIEL *steps out. He is dabbing his
eye with a T-shirt; his head is cut.*

ELLIE. Jesus, what's happened to yer?

MARGARET *marches over to* DANIEL *and grabs his head
in her hands.*

MARGARET. Who did this to yer?

DANIEL *pulls away.*

DANIEL. Oww.

ELLIE. Go easy, Margaret.

MARGARET. Daniel –

DANIEL. Nobody.

> MARGARET *goes to hold his arms.*

> Will yer get off me?

> DANIEL *pulls away and goes to sit on the couch. Everyone is silent for a moment.* ELLIE *sits beside him.*

BOBBY. Are yer all right, Dan?

DANIEL. Yeah.

ELLIE. Daniel, jus' take a deep breath an' tell us like. (*Beat.*) Wha' happened?

DANIEL. Nothin'.

MARGARET. Fuckin' big mess of a nothin'.

ELLIE. Who was it?

DANIEL. No one.

ELLIE. Daniel –

DANIEL. I fell off me bike –

MARGARET. Looks more like a smack to me. Looks like someone's lamped yer good an' proper.

DANIEL. Well it's not.

MARGARET. Someone chasin' yer? Should ring the police . . . little bastards.

ELLIE. Margaret.

DANIEL. I fell over.

ELLIE. Where?

DANIEL. What difference is it?

ELLIE. I'm just askin'.

DANIEL. On the main road.

MARGARET. Yer could have been run over.

ELLIE. How d'yer fall off?

DANIEL. Like anyone falls off. Lost me balance . . . goin' too fast.

MARGARET. Someone chasin' yer?

DANIEL. No.

ELLIE. On the main road?

DANIEL. Yeah.

ELLIE. On yer own?

DANIEL. Yeah.

MARGARET. Yer wanna get somethin' on that. Bit o' TCP . . .
Dettol or somethin'.

MARGARET *goes into the kitchen and starts looking
through the cupboards.*

ELLIE. Where's me da?

DANIEL. Alehouse. Where d'yer fuckin' think?

MARGARET *comes back with a tube of Germolene and
puts some on* DANIEL's *head. He flinches.*

Watch out, will yer, it's sore.

MARGARET. S'what yer get, isn't it, playin' silly buggers.
Could've gone straight under a truck.

DANIEL. Oww.

MARGARET. Take more than a blob of Germolene to sort that
out.

ELLIE. He'll live.

MARGARET. Yer just lost yer balance?

DANIEL *nods.*

Head first?

DANIEL. I butted the kerb.

MARGARET. Did yer?

DANIEL *nods.*

Yer went head first into the kerb and just got a little cut like
that? Head must be made outta rubber or somethin'. Must
be a fuckin' rubber head anyway, arsin' about on the main
road like that.

DANIEL. I wasn't arsin' about.

MARGARET *takes hold of* DANIEL's *face in her hands.*

MARGARET. Tha's gonna be a shiner.

DANIEL *pulls away.*

DANIEL. S'no big deal. Wish yers'd all stop fussin'.

ELLIE. D'yer feel like some tea?

DANIEL. I'm not hungry.

MARGARET. It's deep that, yer know.

DANIEL. I'm all right.

ELLIE. Why yer wantin' to protect vicious little bastards like that, eh?

MARGARET. They want stringin' up, thee do.

BOBBY. They can't go gettin' away with it, yer should –

DANIEL. It was nobody.

BOBBY. Don't be frightened about sayin' anythin'.

DANIEL. Frightened? I'm not fuckin' frightened . . . (*Silence. To* BOBBY.) Fuck off, will yer . . . gi' me some space.

ELLIE. Stop bein' a prick, Dan.

MARGARET. Daniel, don't be like that wi' him, he's just tryin' a be –

BOBBY. You asked me fer tea.

MARGARET. He might have concussion.

DANIEL. I haven't got anythin'. I'm just fuckin' sick o' people stickin' their noses in.

MARGARET. Aah, c'mon now, that's enough.

BOBBY. I wasn't stickin' me nose in.

DANIEL. Fine, well just go, will yer? Go an' not stick yer nose in somewhere else. Sort yer own fuckin' life out 'stead o' messin' wi' everyone else's.

Pause.

BOBBY. Daniel, I don't –

MARGARET. Maybe be a good idea to go, eh son? Come back later, yeah?

BOBBY. Daniel, I'll come back later.

DANIEL. Whatever.

BOBBY *exits, leaving* MARGARET *and* ELLIE *dabbing at* DANIEL'*s head.*

MARGARET. Fell off the bike, me arse.

Scene Thirteen

ANG *stands looking out of the window. After a couple of seconds,* PAUL *comes marching in. He stamps over to the fridge, gets a can of Guinness and takes a swig.*

ANG. Bit early fer that, isn't it? (*Silence.*) Paul.

PAUL. What?

ANG. Bit early fer crackin' open the ale, like.

PAUL. Just . . . leave me alone a sec, will yer, Angela? I'm
   havin' a fuckin' can o' Guiness, not smokin' crack.

ANG. Just had a visitor. (*Silence.*) Paul. (*Beat.*) Some woman's
   just been round. From the school.

   Pause.

PAUL. What's happened?

   Pause.

ANG. Bobby hasn't been goin' in.

PAUL. What?

ANG. He hasn't been goin'.

PAUL. What d'yer mean?

ANG. I mean he's been skivin'.

PAUL. Are thee sure? It's not like he's a big loudmouth is it?
   Keeps a low profile.

ANG. He'd have to keep more than a low profile, Paul. He'd
   have to be fuckin' horizontal.

PAUL. How long?

ANG. Weeks. Missed his first three exams.

PAUL. Fuckin' hell . . . I need this, don't I?

ANG. I'm not exactly thrilled about it meself.

   Pause.

PAUL. Where is he now?

ANG. Is that a trick question? (*Beat.*) Supposedly, he's just
   finished sittin' his Maths exam.

   PAUL *sits down and puts his head in his hands.*

   It was so . . . humiliatin'. Made it worse that she was bein'
   all nice about it. Patronisin', like I'm a bad mother. Me all
   red-faced, tryin' a make light of it . . . 'I'll swing for him
   when he gets home.' 'Oh, I don't think violence is the
   answer, Mrs Thompson.' (*Beat.*) It's a sayin', yer stupid
   stuck-up bitch.

PAUL. How've we not got onto it?

ANG. Coz he's good at blaggin'. (*Beat.*) Like his dad.

The front door goes and we hear the sound of footsteps going upstairs.

PAUL. Right.

ANG. Leave it. (*Shouting.*) Bob.

BOBBY (*offstage*). What?

ANG. Come here.

Pause. Footsteps down the stairs again. BOBBY *enters the kitchen. He looks upset.*

All right. What's up?

BOBBY. Nothin'.

ANG. How'd it go, then?

BOBBY. All right.

ANG. Answer all the questions an' everythin'?

BOBBY. Yeah.

ANG. Glad it's over, yeah?

BOBBY. Mmm.

ANG. Yer don't look it.

BOBBY. I'm just tired.

Silence.

What?

PAUL. Someone's been round, Bob.

BOBBY. Who?

ANG. A truancy officer.

Pause.

BOBBY. How come?

PAUL. Seein' if we want anythin' from the Avon catalogue. Why d'yer think she fuckin' came, Bobby?

ANG. I can't believe it. (*Beat.*) I just . . . I honestly can't –

BOBBY. I told yer, though, (*Beat.*) I said, didn't I?

ANG. Yer told us you were goin' back. (*Beat.*) Gonna do yer exams.

BOBBY. I don't like it. I told yer I didn't like it. (*Beat.*) I don't care about exams.

Silence.

71

PAUL. What's goin' on, Bobby?

BOBBY. What d'you care?

    BOBBY *goes to leave.* PAUL *jumps up and grabs him.*

PAUL. What do I care? I'm yer dad.

BOBBY. Exactly. You're me dad. (*Pause.*) I don't wanna be yer mate. I don't care that yer young. I wish yer weren't young. I just want a normal dad. And I'm sorry to tell yer, Mum, but I don't think I'm gonna be a brain surgeon. Just coz you both gave it all up to have me, doesn't mean that I've gotta go on and do it all for yer.

ANG. I don't want yer to be a brain surgeon.

BOBBY. Whatever. (*Beat.*) Yer want me to be somethin' –

ANG. Is that such a bad thing?

BOBBY. Yer want me to be somethin' for you, not me.

ANG. We want yer to be happy.

PAUL. Make sure that yer okay.

BOBBY. Here we go.

PAUL. Make sure that yer've got everythin' yer need. I'm workin' me balls off, mornin', noon and night. Takin' on extra work. D'yer think I honestly wanna be doin' that?

BOBBY. Don't do it then. I don't ask fer anythin' off yer.

PAUL. Because yer don't need to. (*Beat.*) Yer don't *need* to ask, Bobby, that's the whole point. I'm out there this afternoon, chasing fuckin' Gyppos down the street coz they're nickin' work from under me nose. All so you can fuckin' have stuff.

ANG. Eh, hang on a minute?

BOBBY. What did you just say?

PAUL. Yer've gotta start takin' some sort of responsibility, Bobby –

BOBBY. What did yer just say then about chasin' Gyppos?

PAUL. Don't start changing the fuckin' subject here, mate. Yer were all right at that school. It'd all stopped. No more fuckin' bullies. You promised me and yer mum that –

BOBBY. It was you, wasn't it?

PAUL. It was me what?

BOBBY. You did it.

ANG. Bobby, what are yer on about?

BOBBY. You battered Daniel.

PAUL. Who the fuck's Daniel?

BOBBY. Me best mate.

ANG. From school?

BOBBY. No. From over there. Yer did, didn't yer?

PAUL. Over where?

BOBBY. Curzon Park. He lives on Curzon Park.

ANG. The Traveller site?

PAUL. Yer best mates wi' a Gyppo.

BOBBY. Yer battered him coz yer found him on that job.

ANG. Paul, yer didn't.

BOBBY. Yer did. Yer prick, it was you.

PAUL. No, I didn't . . . only coz the little bastard was too fast
    though. (*Beat.*) Bobby, what the fuck's goin' on?

BOBBY. Why won't yer just admit it?

PAUL. I haven't touched anyone. Bobby, I don't understand
    what's happenin' here.

Silence.

BOBBY. But they're all thieves. That's what I've heard yer
    say . . . time an' time again . . . spongers and thieves.
    They're all on the make . . . see what they can get away
    with. Not like you, eh? Not like you with yer shed chock-a-
    block full o' knock-off from work. Not like you just tryin'
    a' look after yer family. Just coz they choose somethin'
    different that you can't get yer head round. Just coz they
    don't choose four tiny little claustrophobic fuckin' walls in
    a narrow little shitty street. I wish yer hadn't got this house.
    I wish we'd gone off somewhere when I was little, better
    still, I wish I hadn't even been born coz then yer both could
    o' got on with what it was yer really wanted to do. An' you
    wouldn't have to blame it all on me. What a life you
    could've had without a fuckin' weight like me round yer
    neck. No wonder I'm a nervous wreck. Should have
    'burden' tattooed across me forehead.

ANG. That's not fair, that –

BOBBY. It was me anyway. Not Daniel.

PAUL. What d'yer mean?

BOBBY. I told them about the jobs. Thee needed the money. Thee were desperate. You're not.

ANG *stands up and grabs* BOBBY.

ANG. What's the matter with yer, for fuck's sake . . . what's the matter?

PAUL *pulls her off. He sits down and puts his head in his hands.*

PAUL. Why would yer do that to me, Bob? D'yer hate me that much?

BOBBY. No. I love yer. (*Beat.*) But I hate it that yer embarrassed by me. Coz I'm not into clothes or bands or footy an' I don't wanna get paraded round the pub by yer like some little mini you. Sorry I'm such a disappointment. Sorry I make yer both so unhappy.

ANG. Don't say that . . . Yer don't make us unhappy, Bobby, yer don't make –

PAUL. I love you more than I could ever say, Bobby. I'm crippled by it. (*Beat.*) Everything I do. My life . . . is about tryin' to make you happy, Bobby.

BOBBY. Well, why are you two never *ever* happy then . . . if that's what yer want and that's what you try an' do, why isn't this house happy?

ANG. It isn't that simple, Bobby.

BOBBY. I think it is, actually. I think it's simple. I felt happy one time when the three of us went to Rhyll Suncentre and yer didn't argue once and I saw yer kissin' when I wasn't lookin' and the sky was blue and I felt so happy that it almost made me sad. I felt happy when me and Daniel went fishin' in Otterspool last week an' we laughed our heads off about somethin' stupid that we both got and I didn't feel like I didn't belong. Like in school or at home. (*Beat.*) Just little things. It's that simple.

PAUL. There's other stuff goin' on.

BOBBY. What?

ANG. Just . . . stuff. Between me an' yer dad, it's not . . .

PAUL. Private stuff.

BOBBY. Private? Is that right, yeah? D'yer think I'm deaf? (*Beat.*) There's nothin' I don't know about. Walls are made of tracin' paper. I know yer want a baby and you can't have one. I know yer desperate fer a second chance. Have a normal kid. One yer can mould into exactly what yer want. One that doesn't remind yer of all the things yer've missed out on.

PAUL. That's bullshit.

BOBBY. Yer don't even know me.

PAUL *stares at* BOBBY.

Go on. It was me. It was my fault, not Daniel's. (*Beat.*) Give us a thump.

ANG. Jesus Christ.

BOBBY. Go 'ead, yer prick.

Pause. PAUL *stands.* ANG *jumps up.*

ANG. Paul, no –

He walks past BOBBY *and* ANG *to the door.*

PAUL. An' you don't know me. (*Beat.*) Either of yer.

PAUL *leaves.*

Scene Fourteen

Later the same night. The trailer. MARGARET *is sitting up. Someone can be heard fumbling with the door. It takes a few seconds before* FELIX *stumbles in. He's drunk and trying to be quiet. He stumbles toward the bedroom but before he gets there,* MARGARET *switches the light on.* FELIX *stops and turns around.*

FELIX. Wha' you doin there?

MARGARET. Let Daniel have the caravan tonight. (*Beat.*) He needs a bit o' space. (*Silence.*) Job go all right?

FELIX. Aye.

MARGARET. Good night?

FELIX. Not bad.

MARGARET. Where d'yer get to?

FELIX. Here an' there . . . round an' about, y'know.

MARGARET. I don't. No.

FELIX. Well, since it's none o' yer business, I wouldn't worry too much about it.

MARGARET. Nothin' t'me. Yer didn't come back for yer tea, s'all.

FELIX. Sorry, Mammy.

MARGARET. I'm jus' sayin'. Not like you t'miss out where food's concerned.

FELIX. I had chips. (*Beat.*) From the chippy. Can I go now? miss?

Pause.

MARGARET. We had a bit of a drama today.

FELIX. Wa's that?

MARGARET. Daniel.

FELIX. What about him?

MARGARET. Hurt hi'self. Fell over, he says. (*Silence.*) That was some fall, that. Said he went head first onto the kerb. (*Beat.*) Looked more like someone had given him a good thump to me. (*Silence.*) He wouldn't say, though.

Silence.

FELIX. Yer do yer best, yer know, Margaret?

MARGARET. That what yer call it?

FELIX. I do me best.

MARGARET. I'd hate t'see yer worst.

Silence.

FELIX. He deserved it.

MARGARET. God forgive yer.

FELIX. Goodnight, Margaret.

MARGARET. Yer a disgrace. An absolute disgrace. (*Beat.*) She'd be ashamed o' yer.

FELIX. Don't, Margaret.

MARGARET *stands,* FELIX *squares up to her.*

MARGARET. Or what? Eh, Felix? Or what?

Pause. FELIX *sits down.*

FELIX. I keep . . . seein' her. Seein' her face in me head an she's cryin'. (*Pause.*) I thought it was all goin' t' be all right. Like thee said. She'd come home an' she'd be okay an' everythin'd jus' get back t' the way it was. (*Pause.*) The las' time I saw her, I went in . . . took her a bag o' food. Did it all meself. She wa' asleep an' I didn't want t'wake her. y'know? She jus' looked so . . . (*Pause.*) I put the bag down next t'her an kissed her head an' left. I broke me heart when I got outside. Grown man, an' I jus' broke me heart. (*Beat.*) I swore, the next time I saw her in tha' place would be when I wa' gonna get her to bring her home. (*Pause.*) I've let her down so much, haven't I?

MARGARET. No.

FELIX. I don't know what t'do without her. I don't know how t'be . . . Jaysus, I don't know how t'be a person without her, let alone a parent.

MARGARET. Love . . . that's what yer have t'do, Felix . . . jus' give 'em as much love as yer can. Let them make their mistakes.

FELIX. I don't wanna lose everythin', Margaret. I know I'm goin' to. (*Beat.*) I don't want things t'change, yer know.

MARGARET. If yer want things to stay as they are, things have got t'change. Don't be so scared o'lettin' go a bit.

Silence.

FELIX. Yer remind me of her so much, y'know? (*Beat.*) Yer remind me of her so much that I can't bear bein' around yer sometimes. I can't cope wi' yer bein' here. (*Pause.*) I didn't mean it. (*Pause.*) Honestly I jus' didn't mean it but I got so . . . One minute he's standin' there in front o' me givin' me the usual lip an' I'm thinkin' he's spinnin' me one o' his yarns like, an' the next I'm jus' swingin' for him. Really layin' in, like it's all his fault. Everythin'. An' I know she'd be lookin' down an' cryin' her heart out if she saw. An I fuckin' hated him fer that moment. Hated him. Jaysus, like he's not in pieces too. (*Beat.*) I'm so frightened, Margaret, y'know?

MARGARET. I know.

FELIX. Is he all right?

MARGARET. He will be.

Pause.

FELIX. I have this feelin' in me stomach like I wanna turn it all inside out. Like I'm gonna explode or somethin'. (*Beat.*) I have no way of knowin' how to move on. What d'yer do?

MARGARET. Get up every mornin'. Go t'bed every night. And try not t'destroy yerself in between. (*Beat.*) One mornin' yer'll wake up an' yer heart won't be killin' as much as usual. Takes time. (*Silence.*) I'm leavin' in the morning.

FELIX. Back t'sunny Kent.

MARGARET. No. (*Beat.*) I'm not, actually.

FELIX. How d'yer mean?

MARGARET. I got evicted. (*Pause.*) No bother fer a while then outa the blue, bam . . . all over me like vultures. Thrown off of me own land. Coz I haven't got the poxy plannin' permission.

FELIX. Wha' yer gonna do?

MARGARET. I dunno. Get on the road.

Silence.

FELIX. I don't know if I can stay here much longer. Not without Win.

MARGARET. Don't take off but have yer thought about a house?

FELIX. Margaret, I can't be doin' wi' havin' ridiculous conversations wi' yer. (*Beat.*) No matter what yer put on yerself, they'll still know yer. There isn't any point runnin' away from it. Yer'll always be what yer are. It's hard to burn wilderness out of a wild bird's nose.

MARGARET. Birds don't have noses.

FELIX. I'm not livin' in no fuckin' house.

MARGARET. All right . . . I hear yer.

FELIX. Me and Win stayed with Eileen for a bit once. When she got hers. The walls were too thick. Felt like I was in a cement box. I lay in bed at night waitin' to hear the rain on the roof but it never come. S' a terribly lonely sound that, nighttime in a house. Four walls an' lookin' at nothin', only plenty o' bad luck when yer get up. They have prisons fer that sort o' feelin.

Pause.

MARGARET. Daniel's comin' on the road wi' me fer a bit. I spoke t'him an' it's what he wants an' I think it'll do him good, so whatever sort o' fuckin' fuss yer gonna kick up now, there'll be no point. He's comin' an' that's –

FELIX. All right. (*Beat.*) S'all right . . . I'm not sayin' nothin'.

Silence.

MARGARET. He needs some time away. (*Beat.*) I asked Ellie too.

FELIX. What? Margaret –

MARGARET. She's not your wife, she's a young woman. (*Pause.*) As it is, she said no.

FELIX. Did she?

MARGARET. Wants t'stay here. Wi' you.

FELIX. Does she?

MARGARET. Beats me, but there yer go.

FELIX. That's . . . that's something.

MARGARET. Be good t'her.

FELIX. Yes . . . yeah. (*Silence.*) Thank you, Margaret . . . thank you fer comin'.

FELIX *puts his head in his hands.*

Scene Fifteen

ANG *and* BOBBY. BOBBY *watches as* ANG *packs.*

ANG. It's just for a bit. A while.

BOBBY. Where yer gonna go?

ANG. Aunty Kath's. It won't be . . . it's just for a while. I'm not . . . I feel like I'm abandonin' yer . . . yer can come, yer know? If yer want, yer can come with me. It's just for a bit –

BOBBY. I'm gonna stay here.

ANG. All this worryin' about each other –

BOBBY. I'm not a little kid anymore. Yer don't have to worry about me.

ANG. I'll always worry. Yer my son. Yer don't stop. (*Beat.*) You wait till you have kids.

BOBBY. I don't want kids. Too much grief.

ANG. Don't say that.

Silence.

BOBBY. Mum. Have you got a . . . do you have a little box or somethin' that yer keep my things in? Like baby teeth and drawin's . . . school books an' stuff.

ANG. Yeah.

BOBBY. 'Ave yer?

ANG. Of course I have.

BOBBY. What's in it?

Pause. ANG *thinks.*

ANG. Two teeth . . . three teeth. (*Beat.*) A little bag of yer hair
from when you were about four, when it was blonde . . .
A school tie, yer first one with the little bit of lazzy so yer
could just stick it over yer head. That used to make me cry
coz yer'd pull it when you were nervous . . . a letter to me,
a letter to Father Christmas, a letter to yer nan . . . a letter to
Jesus. All the same. All askin' for a dog. Yer first school
photey . . . lots of different things. (*Pause.*) Lots of very
precious things.

BOBBY. Can I look at it?

ANG. Yeah.

ANG *stands but* BOBBY *keeps hold of her hands.*

BOBBY. Not now.

She sits back down.

Just stay here with me for a little bit.

ANG *kisses him on the head.*

ANG. Look after him, won't yer?

BOBBY *nods.*

It won't be fer long.

DANIEL *enters. He hovers in the doorway.* ANG *jumps a
little.*

Jesus. D' thee not have doorbells where you live, Daniel?

DANIEL. No.

BOBBY. Hiya.

DANIEL. It was open.

ANG. It's okay . . . it's all right . . . come in.

DANIEL *comes in and stands there awkwardly.*

(*Taking her bags off a seat.*) Here y'are . . . sit down.

DANIEL *sits. Silence.*

I'll leave yer to it . . . got a few things to do upstairs.
There's some . . . stuff . . . Bobby. Biscuits an' sweets an'
that in the cupboard if yers –

DANIEL. Thanks.

ANG leaves. BOBBY roots through the cupboards. He finds a packet of Kit Kats and throws one to DANIEL.

She off t'hide the ornaments then?

BOBBY laughs.

I like yer house.

BOBBY. Do yer? (*Pause.*) Why?

DANIEL. Just being polite.

BOBBY. Don't be.

Pause. DANIEL puts BOBBY's PS2 on the table.

DANIEL. I'm goin' away for a bit.

BOBBY. Where to?

DANIEL. Wi' Margaret.

BOBBY. How long for?

DANIEL. I dunno. Long as it takes.

BOBBY. Long as what takes?

DANIEL. Till I come back.

Silence.

BOBBY. When yer goin'?

DANIEL. Soon. Day or so.

Pause.

BOBBY. Don't.

DANIEL. Yer can come fer a bit . . . if yer want like. Margaret says.

BOBBY. Really?

DANIEL. Yeah.

Pause.

BOBBY. I can't. (*Silence.*) I had a new one last night.

DANIEL. Jaysus . . . go on.

BOBBY. It was a third world war. They were bombin' all the streets round by ours. Any houses they could see. Looked like it was raining these little black torpedoes. Only place that didn't get hit was the site so we legged it down there . . . dodgin' bombs. Tryin a' get to yours. An' we did, we made it. Then we all piled in.

DANIEL. An' we were safe?

BOBBY. No. Just when we thought it was over, they bombed the trailer n'all.

Scene Sixteen

Curzon Park. The next day. ELLIE *is sitting on the steps of the trailer.* FELIX *walks past her and awkwardly strokes her head as he goes inside.* BOBBY *approaches. He is holding a bunch of flowers.*

ELLIE. Yer shouldn't have.

BOBBY. Sorry. They aren't . . . they're not for you.

ELLIE. Who're they for?

BOBBY. Margaret.

ELLIE. Yer a bit late.

BOBBY. . . .

ELLIE. Thee went last night.

Silence. BOBBY *sits down beside* ELLIE, *clutching the flowers.*

Don't think he's that big on goodbyes. He's a selfish little bastard like that. It's all about him. He left yer somethin'.

ELLIE *goes into the trailer and comes out with a new football. She hands it* BOBBY.

Says yer gotta keep practisin'.

BOBBY. Didn't you wanna go with them?

ELLIE *shrugs.*

ELLIE. Gonna stay here wi' me da fer a while. Look after things. We're gonna join 'em fer a while next month maybe. Have the summer in Ireland.

BOBBY. Sounds boss.

ELLIE. What about you?

BOBBY. I'm goin' to Tenerife.

ELLIE. Wi' yer mam an' da?

BOBBY. Just me dad. They're gettin' divorced. (*Beat.*) I'm absolutely dreadin' it.

ELLIE. I'm sorry –

BOBBY. Oh, I don't mean about that. I mean I'm dreadin'
goin' to Tenerife. (*Beat.*) They should've got divorced years
ago. Only stayed together coz o' me, they reckon. Wish
they'd have asked me what I thought sooner. (*Beat.*) They're
gonna sell the house an' I'm gonna live wi' them both. Take
it in turns. I'm into that, I think. They're better seperate.

ELLIE. Some people are.

BOBBY *stands, he hands the flowers to* ELLIE.

BOBBY. Might as well have these.

ELLIE. Cheers.

BOBBY. See yer.

ELLIE. Bye. (*Pause.*) Bobby. Yer can still come round like,
y'know? Just coz Daniel's gone, doesn't mean . . . yer can
still knock on, if yer want like.

BOBBY. Yeah. I will.

BOBBY *starts to walk off.*

ELLIE. Bobby.

He turns back, ELLIE *runs up to him and hugs him.*

S'off Daniel.

Inside the trailer: FELIX *sits, polishing his work boots.*

The kitchen: ANG *is spraying and wiping down the
countertops. She finishes, puts the spray and cloth away
under the sink. She gets her coat from the back of the door
and leaves.*

The backyard: PAUL *is beginning to build a fire with bits of
wood, he starts emptying the shed and begins to pile boxes
onto the unlit fire.*

BOBBY *enters the kitchen. He goes over to the window and
looks out over Curzon.*

The End.

A Nick Hern Book

The Way Home first published in Great Britain as a paperback
original in 2006 by Nick Hern Books Limited, 14 Larden Road,
London W3 7ST

The Way Home copyright © 2006 Chloë Moss

Chloë Moss has asserted her right to be identified as the author
of this work

Cover image: original photography by Mike Maddox; artwork
by Gavin Lamb

Typeset by Country Setting, Kingsdown, Kent CT14 8ES
Printed in Great Britain by Bookmarque, Croydon, Surrey

A CIP catalogue record for this book is available from
the British Library

ISBN-13   978 1 85459 960 7
ISBN-10   1 85459 960 5